SpringerBriefs in Education

We are delighted to announce SpringerBriefs in Education, an innovative product type that combines elements of both journals and books. Briefs present concise summaries of cutting-edge research and practical applications in education. Featuring compact volumes of 50 to 125 pages, the SpringerBriefs in Education allow authors to present their ideas and readers to absorb them with a minimal time investment. Briefs are published as part of Springer's eBook Collection. In addition, Briefs are available for individual print and electronic purchase.

SpringerBriefs in Education cover a broad range of educational fields such as: Science Education, Higher Education, Educational Psychology, Assessment & Evaluation, Language Education, Mathematics Education, Educational Technology, Medical Education and Educational Policy.

SpringerBriefs typically offer an outlet for:

- An introduction to a (sub)field in education summarizing and giving an overview of theories, issues, core concepts and/or key literature in a particular field
- A timely report of state-of-the art analytical techniques and instruments in the field of educational research
- A presentation of core educational concepts
- An overview of a testing and evaluation method
- A snapshot of a hot or emerging topic or policy change
- An in-depth case study
- A literature review
- A report/review study of a survey
- An elaborated thesis

Both solicited and unsolicited manuscripts are considered for publication in the SpringerBriefs in Education series. Potential authors are warmly invited to complete and submit the Briefs Author Proposal form. All projects will be submitted to editorial review by editorial advisors.

SpringerBriefs are characterized by expedited production schedules with the aim for publication 8 to 12 weeks after acceptance and fast, global electronic dissemination through our online platform SpringerLink. The standard concise author contracts guarantee that:

- an individual ISBN is assigned to each manuscript
- each manuscript is copyrighted in the name of the author
- the author retains the right to post the pre-publication version on his/her website or that of his/her institution

Peter Grootenboer · Christine Edwards-Groves

The Theory of Practice Architectures

Researching Practices

Peter Grootenboer
Griffith Institute for Educational Research
Griffith University
Gold Coast, QLD, Australia

Faculty of Mathematics and Natural Sciences
Universitas Negeri
Malang, East Java, Indonesia

Christine Edwards-Groves
Griffith Institute for Educational Research
Griffith University
Gold Coast, QLD, Australia

ISSN 2211-1921 ISSN 2211-193X (electronic)
SpringerBriefs in Education
ISBN 978-981-99-7349-1 ISBN 978-981-99-7350-7 (eBook)
https://doi.org/10.1007/978-981-99-7350-7

© The Editor(s) (if applicable) and The Author(s), under exclusive license to Springer Nature Singapore Pte Ltd. 2023

This work is subject to copyright. All rights are solely and exclusively licensed by the Publisher, whether the whole or part of the material is concerned, specifically the rights of translation, reprinting, reuse of illustrations, recitation, broadcasting, reproduction on microfilms or in any other physical way, and transmission or information storage and retrieval, electronic adaptation, computer software, or by similar or dissimilar methodology now known or hereafter developed.
The use of general descriptive names, registered names, trademarks, service marks, etc. in this publication does not imply, even in the absence of a specific statement, that such names are exempt from the relevant protective laws and regulations and therefore free for general use.
The publisher, the authors, and the editors are safe to assume that the advice and information in this book are believed to be true and accurate at the date of publication. Neither the publisher nor the authors or the editors give a warranty, expressed or implied, with respect to the material contained herein or for any errors or omissions that may have been made. The publisher remains neutral with regard to jurisdictional claims in published maps and institutional affiliations.

This Springer imprint is published by the registered company Springer Nature Singapore Pte Ltd.
The registered company address is: 152 Beach Road, #21-01/04 Gateway East, Singapore 189721, Singapore

Paper in this product is recyclable.

Preface

By virtue of our involvement in the initial theoretical and empirical introduction of the theory of practice architectures, Peter through his interest and expertise in phenomenology and Christine through her interest and expertise in ethnomethodology, along with our continuing work 'theorising the theory', we are pleased to share with you *The theory of practice architectures: Researching practices*—the book. Along with our amazing colleagues who sat around 'the blue couches' in Wagga Wagga Australia debating theory in the mid-2000s, we were, at once, novices to the conceptual ideas we were coproducing. But through our own long-standing research collaboration and shared scholarship, we believe it is timely to make good on our promise (and in the spirit of the blue lounge methodology) to support others in the continued understanding, utility, and development of the theory.

This book—*The theory of practice architectures: Researching practices*—responds and contributes to the growing use of the theory to explain and critique social phenomena. The intention is to, firstly, respond and speak to the growing number of researchers across the world coming to the theory for the first time and interested in considering the theory of practice architectures for their own empirical research; and secondly, contribute to the body of existing work by explaining, synthesising, and critiquing the principal conceptual resources that comprise the theory. A main purpose for us is to support researchers study practices by providing further insights, perhaps suggestions, into understanding, connecting, situating, analysing, interpreting, and reporting practices (as reflected in the organisation of the book) as framed by the theory of practice architectures.

If you have picked up this book, then, we are assuming, you are interested in practices, and the potential of the theory of practice architectures to illuminate and explain the particularity and distinctiveness of practices of the kind you are interested in or challenged by. Across the world, and in ranging social fields like education, health, and business, the theory has been put to work, theoretically and empirically, to understand how practices get done in the day-to-day personal and professional lives of people. As our dear friend and colleague Stephen Kemmis reminds us, *we live our life in practices*—practices that flow through and from *the everyday* (like preparing an evening meal or shopping), to *the professional* (like in careers such as teaching or medicine), to *the highly specialised* (like a meeting with your financial advisor or managing an evacuation), or to *the unpredictability of happenstance* (like calling the ambulance in a medical emergency or finding shelter in a storm). Coming to practices over the courses of our lives, days, or moments, involves participating—and thus, and entering or joining existing *practicescapes* that are always dynamic, overlapping, interspersed, and evolving.

The ubiquity of the word 'practice' in professional, political, and research parlance has raised the need for us to put the spotlight on *practice* itself—not just in a theoretical sense, but in the empirical study of it (through a focus on formulating practice-oriented research questions and designing practice-based research). As we illustrate in this book, as a basic notion, the study of practices (whatever your discipline or field of concern or interest) realises that they 'continually unfold' in activity flowing through *sayings* in words, thoughts and language, through *doings* in time and in spaces, through *relatings* in roles and relationships, and that this activity *as it happens* involves persons simultaneously interpreting, negotiating, and mediating the situations they find themselves in *then and there*. In general terms, this essentialises the need in practice-based research to closely examine what *is* happening, to supplement how practitioners might account for what is happening. The theory of practice architectures assiduously attends to *happenings*, thus always pays attention, is even highly sensitive, to (i) *the site*—simply because practices always happen somewhere, (ii) *the sociality*—simply because practices happen with, between and because of people; and (iii) *the semantic*—simply because practices must be understood or comprehensible in the here-and-now activity, and be able to be described and explained subsequently in other occasions of practising (by participants and researchers alike). As we see it, this sets out the basis impetus for the using the theory of practice architectures and guides the principles for its use in critical ethnographic research, for example.

Guiding Principles

As we have written elsewhere (see, e.g., Edwards-Groves & Grootenboer, 2023; Kemmis et al., 2014), from its genesis, the theory of practice architectures has aligned with three central principles: (i) a *theoretical, and thus linguistic, principle* that aims to articulate a theoretical language that can be used to interpret and describe the social world; (ii) a *critical principle* that aims to identify ways in which current practices reasonably and/or unreasonably, justly and/or unjustly and productively and/or unproductively enable and/or constrain individual and collective *self-expression, self-development*, and *self-determination*[1]; and (iii) a *practical and transformative principle* that aims to facilitate the development—and so transformation in real and practical terms—of practices in times of increasing instability and rapid change to social,

---

[1] Informed by the work of Iris Marion Young (1990) who described justice and injustice in terms of these three ideas: self-expression, self-development, and self-determination.

environmental, economic, cultural, and political circumstances, as experienced in particular sites across the globe. These principles cohere around the fundamental view, that, as we wrote with our colleagues (Kemmis et al., 2014, p. 6):

> we cannot transform practices without transforming existing arrangements in the intersubjective spaces that support the conduct of practices.

And so, idealistically, the theory of practice architectures provides an inherently practical opening move to address questions about the extent to which a 'theory' can also be a mechanism for practical transformation, as we will show in this book. This position was explained earlier by Kemmis et al. (2014, p. 6) in their seminal book *Changing practices, changing education*:

> We cannot transform practices without composing new ways of understanding the world, making it comprehensible in new discourses; without constructing new ways of doing things, produced out of new material and economic arrangements; and without new ways of relating to one another, connecting people and things in new social and political arrangements—all 'bundled together' in new projects of schooling for education. This is the task of transformation.

Over time, the transformative aspiration of the theory of practice architectures emerged as a notable and continuing contribution that seeks to fulfil the broad promises of research regardless of the field of study. Central to this view is the idea that—*since practices happen, they can, and always will be changed*. The theory of practice architectures provides a stereoscopical pivot point from which to interpret, critique and, ultimately, transform practices. On this count, the theory of practice architectures provides an important organising conceptual framework (or even a mapping tool) for researchers, like us, studying the enabling and constraining conditions that benefits (or not) individuals and societies. For us, keeping these principles alive and central to the core of our own work means understanding that the theory of practice architectures offers the researcher practical ways to (i) think about and describe practices and the practice architectures that influence them, (ii) critique practices and practice architectures, and (iii) consider how to change practices and practice architectures vis-à-vis drawing out the implications of research findings in practical ways that speak to practitioners, policy-makers, and researchers alike.

A Brief History[2]

We believe understanding the genealogy of the theory helps theorists themselves come to deeper understandings of its core conceptual underpinnings. Put simply,

---

[2] In the 2017 book 'Exploring education and professional practice', edited by Mahon, Francisco, and Kemmis, a more detailed timeline and history of the theoretical influences that, from Stephen Kemmis' perspective, contributed to the development of the theory of practice architectures is outlined by their interview-style chapter by Kemmis and Mahon (2017), Chapter 13 'Coming to practice architectures: a genealogy of the theory' (p. 219–239).

the theory of practice architectures did not simply appear from the ether, we see it as a radical constellation of ideas informed by a broad number of theoretical propositions. Like practices themselves, the practice of conceptualising the theory of practice architectures was prefigured by the histories of the particular practitioners (a group of Australian educational researchers at Charles Sturt University of which we were part) who came together in 2006, in the home of Stephen Kemmis and Roslin Brennan Kemmis, to grapple with contemporary issues challenging education and educational research. As our discussions unfolded, and as we bounced around ideas and theories, we were influenced by the semantic (theoretical discourses), physical (sitting in a home on blue lounge chairs), and relational (a group of colleagues) conditions we encountered at that time.

Early conceptualisations evolved organically through robust theoretical, critical, and philosophical discussions between Stephen Kemmis, Tracy Smith, Peter Grootenboer, Christine Edwards-Groves, Helen Russell, Ian Hardy, Jane Wilkinson, Roslin Brennan Kemmis, and William Adlong, who from their different intellectual traditions (practical philosophy, critical theory, phenomenology, ethnomethodology, sociology, critical hermeneutics), theoretical orientations (including Bourdieu, Garfinkle, Habermas, Marx, MacIntyre, Schatzki, Vygotsky, Wittgenstein[3]), and disciplines (mathematics and literacy education, higher education, vocational education, leadership, environmental education), convened because of a shared interest in and commitment to education practices, to ask questions about practice, and its conceptual, theoretical, and practical dimensions (see Footnote 3 below for a further list of significant theorists that informed the earlier work). At that time, as a group of scholars, we were intent on understanding and 'speaking back' to the crosscurrents and issues in education policy and neoliberal management being experienced by educators at that time. This interest-in-common gave rise to the establishment of regular meetings among our group, that convened on the blue couches, to critique the history of, and developments in, practice theory and philosophy (and to eat Rozzie's home-cooked curries and cake). Discussions about the convergences and divergences, affordances and shortcomings of the varying standpoints, the conceptual leanings of the different theoretical perspectives presented in a burgeoning body of social practice literature generated what we see as a conceptually rich palette of ideas. These ideas translated into the foundations for the theory of practice architectures.

To capitalise on the benefits of these early discussions that included in person conversations with Wilfred Carr and Theodore Schatzki, and to what practice theorists Schatzki, Knorr Cetina, and Savigny (2001) described as 'the practice turn' in social life and organisational activity, the 2008 book *Enabling Praxis: Challenges for Education* (edited by Stephen Kemmis and Tracey Smith) was published. *Practice architectures* was put to work empirically in chapters by each of the contributors in relation to their different fields of study, but it was the chapter *Situating praxis*

---

[3] For example, discussions took place about works by Bourdieu 1990, 1998; Carr 2007; Carr & Kemmis 1986; Garfinkle 1967; Gherardi 2008; Green 2009; Habermas 1987; Hadot, 1995; Kemmis 2009; Lave & Wenger 1991; MacIntyre 1981; Marx; Reckwitz 2002; Schatzki 1996, 2002, 2010; Schatzki, Knorr-Cetina & von Savigny 2001; Shotter 1996; Vygotsky 1976; and Wittgenstein 1958, 1975, 1980.

in practice: Practice architectures and the cultural, social and material conditions for practice written by Stephen Kemmis and Peter Grootenboer (2008) that first presented the detailed theoretical propositions of the theory. This period coincided with the early days of the international 'Pedagogy Education and Praxis' (PEP established in 2006) research network[4] where initial conceptualisations of the theory were tested and shared with colleagues through a range of publications, but also in international seminars, workshops, and conference presentations. It was through this early dissemination work, particularly through feedback, further reflection and discussion with PEP colleagues, that the theory was refined and applied.

A critical phase in the historical development of the theory of practice architectures was the three-year empirical study *Leading and learning: Developing ecologies of educational practice*, funded by the Australian Research Council (2010–2012) that built on preliminary work of the earlier research undertaken in 2009 by the team Stephen Kemmis, Christine Edwards-Groves, Peter Grootenboer, Ian Hardy, and Jane Wilkinson. The empirical significance of the leading and learning study for the development of the theory of practice architectures was 'recognising the interdependence of [different] kinds of [education] practices [that] prompted the development of our theory of ecologies of practices' (Kemmis et al., 2014, p.13–15). Specifically, ecological relationships were found in dynamic traceable connections between the five education practices of (a) student learning, (b) teaching, (c) teacher learning, (d) leading, and (e) research and reflection (we described as meta-practices at the time). This cluster was named the *Education Complex of Practices* (or the Education Complex) that has remained a key idea in the practice architectures lexicon. Observing and reporting the empirical nature of these relationships 'in practices and practice architectures' was critical for instating the notable contribution that the theory could make to educational research. The detailed description of the empirical, analytical, and theoretical developments of the theory of practice architectures, like the conceptualisation of ecologies of practices, was subsequently published in the text *Changing practices, changing education* (2014) co-authored by the research team (Stephen Kemmis, Jane Wilkinson, Christine Edwards-Groves, Ian Hardy, Peter Grootenboer and Laurette Bristol). Significantly, the use and validity of the theory was substantiated and strengthened by the intensely empirical basis of the work reported and remains the seminal work for researchers studying practices and education. Added to this, what this timeline hints at, but does not explicitly show, is a prolonged and deep period of dialogue and critical reflection supported by engagement with a range of seminal texts authored by notable philosophers, sociologists, linguists and critical theorists (noted above); but, at the same time, grounded in empirical data.

A testament to the ongoing significance to educational research is the prevalence of the theory of practice architectures disseminated in research conducted by scholars involved in the international PEP research network investigating a range of topics and

---

[4] The Pedagogy, Education and Praxis research network (PEP) was established in 2006, and currently involves researchers from Australia, Canada, Colombia, Finland, New Zealand, Norway, South Africa, Sweden, The Netherlands, The United Kingdom, and Trinidad & Tobago.

issues in contemporary education, health and environmental sustainability. Increasingly, PEP researchers, among scholars from a range of diverse national contexts and intellectual traditions from every continent of the world, have published empirical research that utilises the theory of practice architectures to interpret the unique circumstances they observe in their own countries. Among these works are a number of edited volumes presenting collaborative international research that explores, compares, and critiques education practices and practice architectures within and across different national contexts.[5]

This brief history illustrates that *the theory of practice architectures* was developed discursively, dialogically, and practically over a number of years—predominantly by the original 'blue lounge' scholars. By and large, however, the requisite concepts forming the core of the theory of practice architectures, as published in the book *Changing practices, changing education* (2014), have largely remained unchanged. Although, as time has passed, the core ideas have been refined, deepened, and translated, and recast in new social fields inasmuch as the theory transcends the circumstances and conditions of education (where it begun). That said, the theory remains open to critique and further refinement—thus is, at once, dynamic, critical, and evolving. To which we maintain the theory itself is open to evolution in a process of ongoing transformation as new conversations, new theoretical propositions, and new conditions for practices are encountered and discussed. What is perhaps most important to appreciate from this brief historical account is that the theory is philosophically and empirically grounded.

The concepts we present in this book about the theory of practice architectures have a long history of consideration, application, and evolution, but the 2014 book *Changing practices, changing education* remains the most authoritative. Yet there are still many concepts used in conjunction with the theory that remain less clearly understood, such as the relationship between 'practices and practice architectures', and 'enabling and constraining', and 'theory of practice architectures and the theory of ecologies of practices'; and questions still asked about the theory's consideration of agency, intersubjectivity, site ontological perspectives, the complex of practices, site-based education development and analysing practices—on these points we hope

---

[5] International research using the practice architectures has appeared in many journals, and co-edited and co-authored volumes (in English) including: *Enabling Praxis: Challenges for Education* (Kemmis & Smith, 2008, Sense); *Pedagogy Education and Praxis* (Smith, Edwards-Groves & Brennan Kemmis, Eds, 2015, Pedagogy Culture and Society); *Professional Development: Education for ALL as praxis* (Wilkinson, Bristol & Ponte, Eds, 2016); *Practice theory perspectives on pedagogy and education* (Grootenboer, Edwards-Groves & Choy, Eds, 2017, Springer), *Exploring education and professional practice* (Mahon, Francisco & Kemmis, Eds, 2017, Springer), *Education in an Era of Schooling* (Edwards-Groves, Grootenboer & Wilkinson, Eds, 2018, Springer); *Partnership and recognitions in action research* (Edwards-Groves, Olin & Karlberg-Granlund, Eds, 2017 Educational Action Research; 2019, Palgrave); *Pedagogy, education, and praxis in critical times* (Mahon et al., Eds, 2020, Springer); *Middle leadership in schools* (Grootenboer, Edwards-Groves & Rönnerman, 2020, Routledge); *Generative Leadership* (Edwards-Groves & Rönnerman, 2021, Springer); *Living well in a world worth living in* (Reimer, Kaukko, Windsor, Mahon & Kemmis, Eds, 2023, Springer). It is important to note that research using the theory is published in a range of languages including Finnish, Swedish, and Spanish.

the book offers some clarity in answering questions related to these. However, the chapter 'Roads not travelled, roads ahead: How the theory of practice architectures is travelling' by Kemmis, Wilkinson and Edwards-Groves (2017, pp 239–256) comprehensively fleshes many of these ideas out (so that text is very helpful for the reader who wishes to explore the ideas further).

As a reader of the theory, we fully appreciate your work in reading this book (like all books outlining theory) is one of interpretation of, and interaction with, our authorial ideas, thus it is a largely a linguistic or hermeneutic exercise. The chapters that follow present detailed descriptions of the characterising features that form the conceptual machinations of practice architectures. On this, we hope that our writing untangles the complex machinery of the theory of practice architectures by making these (complex) ideas accessible and not overly complicated—and, at the same time, not losing sight of their close interrelationship and interdependence. So that from that standpoint, we hope that whatever your own intellectual and language background that you are respectfully accommodated—where necessary, footnotes provide additional information, or examples provide practical illustrations or explanations. An *annotated glossary* of key concepts and terms is also provided as an appendix to offer the reader additional points of reference to the lexicon that comprises the theory of practice architectures. This text, along with the annotated glossary, aims to carry forward the central conceptual ideas, particularly as regards to their utility in the development and interpretation of empirically grounded, practice-oriented research.

Gold Coast, Australia Peter Grootenboer
Christine Edwards-Groves

Acknowledgements

Together, we both wish to acknowledge our 'blue lounge' colleagues and friends, who through our early collaborative endeavours critiquing theory and practice came to the theory of practice architectures. We recognise and appreciate our ongoing collaboration and intellectual kinship with Karin Rönnerman and Kirsten Petri, especially in relation to our international middle leading research. We recognise scholars in the international Pedagogy Education and Praxis (PEP) who, from the outset, tussled with the conceptual ideas proposed by the theory of practice architectures, listened to us, challenged us, critiqued our work, and engaged with us as interlocutors making sense of the theory as it was put to work in research. But we especially thank Stephen Kemmis for sharing his intellect, and his ongoing mentorship, warm generosity, and infectious enthusiasm for developing and strengthening the theory of practice architectures.

Christine would like to particularly acknowledge the unwavering support from her family, especially Rob, Jessica, Thomas, and Madeline. Thank you.

Peter would like to thank his family and friends for their ongoing support and encouragement, and for keeping him 'grounded', especially Ange, Jake, Danneke, Tilly, Mikey, Phil, Nicole, and Rob.

Contents

1 **Understanding Practices, Practice Architectures, and Practicescapes: The Theory of Practice Architectures** 1
   1.1 The Affordances of Practice Theories: A Brief Overview 2
   1.2 Practices 5
      1.2.1 The Project of a Practice 7
   1.3 Practice Architectures 9
      1.3.1 Making Sense of Practice Arrangement Bundles 11
   1.4 Practicescapes: A Site Ontological, Historical, and Ecological Framing 12
      1.4.1 Historical Framings 13
      1.4.2 Ecological Framings 14
      1.4.3 Site Ontological Framings 14
   1.5 The Theory of Practice Architectures 16
      1.5.1 Arrangements 17
      1.5.2 Interspatial Dimensions 18
      1.5.3 An Example 18
      1.5.4 The Theory of Practice Architectures and Other Theories 19
   1.6 Overcoming Practice Theory and Individual–Social Dualisms 20
      1.6.1 The Challenge of a Site Ontological Practice Approach 21
   1.7 Conclusion 22
   References 23

2 **Connecting Practices: The Theory of Ecologies of Practices** 25
   2.1 Ecologies of Practices as Related to Practice Architectures 27
   2.2 The 'Ecological' Arrangement 28
      2.2.1 Ecological Interdependencies 29
   2.3 A 'Practice Complex' 33
      2.3.1 The Education Complex of Practices 34
      2.3.2 The Implications for Research 36
   2.4 Conclusions 38
   References 39

3	**Situating Practices: A Site Ontological Perspective to Study Design**		41
	3.1 Site Ontologies and Social Practices		42
	3.2 What is Site Ontology?		43
		3.2.1 Three Senses of Site	44
		3.2.2 Why is Site Ontology Vital to Practice Theory?	45
		3.2.3 How Do We Reconcile a 'Theory' with a Site Ontological Perspective?	46
	3.3 Researching Practices in Sites		47
	3.4 Designing Practice-Based Research		48
		3.4.1 Situating Practice—Implications for Data Gathering	48
		3.4.2 Actuality of Practice	49
		3.4.3 Artefacts of Practice	50
		3.4.4 Accounts of Practice	51
		3.4.5 Some Words of Caution	52
		3.4.6 Research Design	53
		3.4.7 Research Questions	53
		3.4.8 Research Methodologies	54
	3.5 Concluding Comments		55
	References		56
4	**Studying Practices: Interpreting and Analysing Data**		57
	4.1 Interpreting Practices as Practical Activity in the World		58
		4.1.1 The Complexity of Interpreting Practices in Sites: Practice Inside Out	59
	4.2 Analysis of Practices		60
		4.2.1 Examples of Analytic Approaches	62
	4.3 Conclusion		74
	Appendix 1: Table of Invention: An Example of Cells (Kemmis et al., 2014, p. 226)		75
	References		76
5	**Reporting Practices: Research Dissemination for Transformation**		79
	5.1 Navigating the Complexities for Presenting Coherent Portrayals of Practices: Untangling the Problem of Practice		81
		5.1.1 Capturing Analytic Distinctions Amidst Empirical Cohesion	82
		5.1.2 Example 5.1	83
		5.1.3 Implementing an Impactful Transformative Dissemination Strategy	85
		5.1.4 The Theory of Practice Architectures: Research for Transformation	87
	5.2 Conclusion		91
	References		91

Appendix 1: Annotated Glossary 93

Index 101

Chapter 1
Understanding Practices, Practice Architectures, and Practicescapes: The Theory of Practice Architectures

Abstract This chapter presents the theory of practice architectures as a social practical and critical theory for understanding practices, practice architectures, and practicescapes. The theory is located in a broad family of practice theories which typically seek to explain society, culture, and human interactions within the social, material, and semantic world. The chapter focuses on the affordances of the theory of practice architectures' constituent conceptual resources. This includes describing and explaining the three composite realms of social practice including sayings, doings, and relatings; the practice architectures which form enabling and constraining conditions and found in site-based cultural–discursive, material–economic, and social–political arrangements; and the three interdependent dimensions of intersubjective space encountered in semantic, physical space–time and social spaces. The ways that theory of practice architectures attends empirically to matters arising from three interrelated multifocal lenses framing the historical, ecological, and site ontological features of a *practicescape* are discussed. Since the theory is interested in matters of human sociality, the chapter draws out concepts concerning human interactivity, meaning making and discourse, knowing in practice, activity, the body and things in practice, human agency, power, and the vested interests of practitioners. To conclude, the challenges for taking a site ontological rather than a predominantly epistemological research stance are addressed.

This chapter presents the main conceptual ideas encompassing the theory of practice architectures. The theory is one which seeks to put practice at the centre of focus, but at the same time alleviate the incessant overuse and glossing of the term 'practice' expressed in catch-all constructs like 'best practice', 'professional practice', or 'literacy practice' by outlining a socially situated and more nuanced view of practice. In social fields such as education, health, business, or even agriculture, the word practice is widely used, even taken as a priori, to describe the (so-called) generally understood practical ways the work of educators, health carers, business managers or agriculturalists (for instance) gets done. As Green (2009, p. 2) remarked,

> *practice* is a term that circulates incessantly, and seems constantly and sometimes even compulsively in use, without always meaning much at all. Rather, it seems to float across the

surface of our conversations and our debates, never really thematised and indeed basically unproblematised, a 'stop-word' par excellence. So it is important to be clear at the outset that practice is not simply the Other of terms and concepts such as 'theory' or 'policy', as conventional usage would have it, though it might be linked in interesting ways to them.

In response to the propensity to take for granted its meaning and utility in everyday vernacular as pointed out here by Green, the chapter begins by problematising the more generalised notions of 'practice' in terms of how it is understood in the theory of practice architectures. Specifically, the chapter aims to provide clarity, detail, and coherence to the reader's understandings of practice and practice architectures, and to practice theories in general; noting, we recognise that in the attempt to offer such clarity and detail to the conceptual resources which comprise the theory, that for explanatory and illustrative purposes we draw apart the undeniably interconnected component parts from their more comprehensive whole.

The chapter is organised in three main sections seeking to answer these basic, but interrelated questions: what are practice theories? what are practices? what are practice architectures? The first section will provide an overview of practice theories in general, and more specifically how the theory of practice architectures is located within the broader social research field. The second section describes examines *practices*. The third section explains *practice architectures* by elaborating its key concepts as initially introduced by Kemmis and Grootenboer (2008) and elaborated by Kemmis et al. (2014a, 2014b).

1.1 The Affordances of Practice Theories: A Brief Overview

The theory of practice architectures is one from a body of practice theories aligned with the social sciences and located in, and drawing from, the broad fields of *anthropology* (disciplined inquiry focused on culture, individuals, and their behaviours[1]), *philosophy* (mainly focused on understanding the meanings of phenomena through ethics, logic, and physics and variously centred on morality, reason and reality, politics, and materialism[2]), and *sociology* (disciplined inquiry mainly focused on the social world and sociality, and the consequences of human action on one another and the environment[3]). However, a unified prescribed theory of practice does not exist, since, by and large, they derive their particular and nuanced emphasis from across the spectrum of theoretical positions, historical influences, and indeed, from each

---

[1] Among the notable anthropologists are Boaz 1858–1942; Mead 1901–1978; Strauss 1908–2009; Latour 1947–2022; Goodall 1934–Present; Strathern 1941–Present.

[2] Among the notable philosophers are the ancient Greek triad Socrates 469–399 BCE, Plato 428–348 BCE and Aristotle 384–322 BCE; Confucius 551–479 BCE; Voltaire 1694–1778; Rousseau 1712–1778; Kant 1724–1804; Wollstonecraft 1759–1797; Wittgenstein 1889–1951; Foucault 1926–1984; Habermas 1929–Present.

[3] Among the notable sociologists are Marx 1818–1883; Martineau 1802–1876; Bourdieu 1930–2002; Goffman 1922–1982; Garfinkel 1917–2011.

other. This suggests the need for overtly recognising and so explicating the 'how contingencies of these [historic] processes continue to shape the present' (Garland, 2014, p. 371). Therefore, practice theories should be approached as a plurality. As Nicolini (2012, p. 1) says, they 'constitute, in fact, a rather broad family of theoretical approaches connected by a web of historical and conceptual similarities' where 'much is to be gained, if we appreciate both the similarities and differences among practice theories, and if we make such differences work for us'.

Practice theories emerged predominantly in the twentieth century to explain society, culture, and human interactions within the social, physical, and semantic world. Schatzki (2001) notably described this theoretical movement as a 'practice turn', where the theorist by-and-large turns their gaze towards the specificity of the conduct of practice. Thus, the turn towards a focus on practice is necessarily concerned with a deeply ethnographic interest in the human condition. As Kemmis (2021, p. 7) recently said,

> The unique power of practice theory is that it addresses *what happens*: how life unfolds – and how practices unfold – in the intersubjective spaces in which we encounter one another and the world, in what Schatzki describes as 'the plenum of practices' (emphasis added).

Here, as Kemmis, Schatzki, and others insist, the site figures prominently. Taking these ideas together, practices are influenced by sites, and reciprocally, sites influence practices. Therefore, many practice theories orient to a site ontological view about what happens, and so happening and *happeningness* (Edwards-Groves & Grootenboer, 2023; Kemmis et al., 2014a, 2014b; this concept is explained later in this chapter and in more detail in Chap. 3).

In general terms, practice theories commonly purport a sensitivity to the social, which at the same time, attempt to remedy or even dissolve tendencies of describing the world in terms of 'irreducible dualisms between actor/system, social/material, body/mind, and theory/action' (Nicolini, 2012, p. 2). Specifically, this theoretical impetus seeks to illuminate the distinctive yet interconnected realities of universal organisational structures and individual agency—putting into view the importance of the interrelationship between the individual and the collective. It is in this vein that the interest in practice theories largely attends to ways the vast arrays of social activity interconnect and overlap as these pass-through time and place, seeking to enlighten understandings about social production and reproduction as the practices that constitute this activity are made and remade anew on each occasion of practising (Bourdieu, 1990; Ingold, 2011). For practice theorists, therefore, occasions of practising involve the individual agent as an active participant in the formation and reproduction of their social world carrying and carrying out social practices as they interact with others and the world (Edwards-Groves & Freebody, 2021; Reckwitz, 2002).

Practice theories, in general, have the capacity to resonate with the contemporary experience and the organisation of social life with benefits lying in their 'capacity to describe important features of the world we inhabit as something that is routinely made and re-made in practice using tools, discourse and our bodies' (Nicolini, 2012, p. 10). But it is through a particular 'standpoint' that researchers examine practices in terms of its capacity to illuminate the details of the day-to-day activity that bring meaning, substance, and purpose to human social life. In summarising the affordances of the broad assemblage of practice theories, Nicolini (2012, pp. 3–6) foregrounds some basic conceptual resemblances and resonances among them; these include an interest in studying:

- *human interactivity* (thus an interest in the social, interactional, and relational),
- *knowledge, meaning, and discourse* (thus an interest in cognition, language and ways of knowing, learning, communicating, sensemaking, and participating discursively),
- *the body and things* (thus an interest in ways humans engage with the materials and objects 'in play' in the physical space),
- *activity* (thus an interest in temporality and processes where practices are understood as perpetually in motion),
- *the agent and agency* (thus an interest in an individual's initiative, creativity, adaptability, responsivity, and performance), and
- *power and the vested interests of practitioners* (thus an interest in privilege, conflict, politics, tension, and solidarity).

Different practice theories variously take account, to greater or lesser extents, of these focal points of interest in their capacity to describe distinctive features of everyday practice. Importantly each theory is informed by its own standpoint on practice involving different intellectual traditions, histories, idiom, or vocabularies, and sets of principal assumptions that underlie their capacity to inform the study, interpretation, description, explanation and analysis of various aspects of social life. Thus, approaching the study of practice not only requires a particular practice lens (Mahon et al., 2017) or practice standpoint (sometimes described by researchers as a practice framing, practice sensibility, practice disposition, practice positioning, practice stance, practice perspective, practice idiom, or practice-based approach), but also the strategic, deterministic, and deliberate selection of a particular theory to guide the particular research design (as we will discuss in subsequent chapters).

However, we caution that simply jumping on the *practice bandwagon* (as described by Corradi et al., 2010) falls prey to criticisms of the blind overuse of the term 'practice' (and its composite features) unless the researcher takes seriously the theoretical nuances, conceptual resources, and empirical demands that the different theories bring to bear on the specific study they are pursuing. This is necessary since a token application of selected concepts as a symbolic gesture towards adopting a practice lens, or using a particular conceptual idiom that the 'lens' might offer, is not enough. Put simply, this is because the risk is an oversimplification or blurring of the theoretical, conceptual, and empirical lines offered by the particular theory. This is a *researcherly* task involving fidelity and clarity that requires explicit explanations of the theoretical, interpretive, and analytic methods and instruments applied be made (not demeaning a researcher's creativity to innovate theory through approaching their study as bricolage—since this is how the theory of practice architectures emerged and continues to be refined, questioned, and critiqued, see, e.g., Hopwood, 2021). Hence, the imperative to 'question ruthlessly those instruments'

(Bourdieu & Wacquant, 1992, p. 249) must remain a priority. The theory of practice architectures is but one practice theory; and this book draws out the principal assumptions and conceptual resources necessary for theorising and analysing practices from the perspective of the theory of practice architectures. The next section focuses on the key interest of practice theory—practices.

1.2 Practices

The practice theorist is interested, in the main, in where, what, and how practices happen as people (practitioners of practices) come together in social activities with varying degrees of expertise, experience, accountabilities, and interest. So, what is a practice? As Wenger (1998, p. 47) said, a 'practice is doing, but not just doing in and of itself. It is doing in historical and social context that gives structure and meaning to what people do. In this sense, practice is always social practice'. In this vein, giving meaning and structure to what people do in their everyday routine social lives requires understanding the organisation and sensemaking involved in the doing of activity, that at the same time involves people in different kinds of relationships communicating with one another around the practice-in-common or the project of the practice (described later). Therefore, people come to practices as interlocutors, meeting in and around *ordinary everyday, professional, specialised,* or *serendipitous* situations. These situations multifariously involve practices comprised of informality, formality, routine, and happenstance, and that these shift discursively, temporally and intersubjectively across the course of a practice and as people move between practices in their daily activity. It is in and across the ever-changing day-to-day moment-by-moment situations as people live their lives, where people say things, do things and relate to others and the world around them.

Therefore, at a most rudimentary level, the theory of practice architectures posits that practices constitute everyday mundane human activity (be it at home, at school, at work, or engaging in community activities such as sport or shopping). In their activity, practices are always characterised by the three entwined socially constituted activities consisting of *sayings, doings,* and *relatings* as interrelated realms of practising. According to the theory of practice architectures, it is in the nexus of the composite activity of sayings, doings, and relatings that practices can be understood, where *activity* itself is a 'temporalspatial event' (Schatzki, 2010, p. 171) brought to life by sayings, doings, and relatings. Specifically, the term *sayings* refers to ideas communicated discursively and interpreted in characteristic and coherent forms of understanding, speaking, and thinking; *doings* refers to things done in characteristic modes of action, activity, and interactivity; and *relatings* refers to the characteristic ways individuals in their activity and interactivity relate to one another and the world around them. It is important to make the distinction here that practices are not activities in and of themselves, but always co-ordinated in ever-present sayings, doings, and relatings simultaneously mobilised in the time–space of human activity. In this sense, practices are dynamic and always in motion discursively and relationally across time and space.

Practices, too, are coherent in the sense that what is happening at a particular place at a particular time is understood (to varying degrees) by or made comprehensible to those present in the activity of practising and according to the particular occasion of practising (e.g., in a lesson where teaching and learning are taking place; in a consultation between a doctor and a patient; in a meeting between the accountant and their client). As a guide to empirical observation, the focus turns to examining how participants in a practice (like teachers, students, doctors, patients, accountants, or clients) negotiate *and* display their understanding about how to participate (in the lesson, consultation, or meeting) in terms of the relevance and appropriateness of the take up and use of particular *sayings* (evident in what is actually being said at the time), particular *doings* (evident in what is actually being done at the time), and particular *relatings* (evident in how the people present are actually relating to one another at the time) that contribute to the co-ordinated and coherent organisation of the practice (being enacted at the time). Taking these core ideas together, Kemmis et al. (2014b, p. 26) arrived at this definition of practice,

> A practice is a form of socially established cooperative human activity in which characteristic arrangements of actions and activities (doings) are comprehensible in terms of arrangements of relevant ideas in characteristic discourses (sayings), and when the people and objects involved are distributed in characteristic arrangements of relationships (relatings), and when this complex of sayings, doings and relatings 'hangs together' in a distinctive project.

This definition follows ideas also expressed by MacIntyre (1981, p. 187) who said that practice is "a coherent and complex form of socially established co-operative human activities". Here, social coherence is accomplished and displayed in practices as people encounter one another in practices; a concept that focuses most particularly on the complex relationship between individuals and groups of individuals (or practitioners) and their shared participation (as interlocutors) in practices. It can be understood as being a relationship in which participants

(i) communicate in language characteristic of the practice they are participating in (the typical and/or expected *sayings associated with, e.g., teaching, learning, health, or accountancy*),
(ii) engage in activities of the practice in physical set-ups and material objects characteristic of that practice (the typical and/or expected *doings associated with, e.g., teaching, learning, health, or accountancy*), and
(iii) enter relationships with other people and objects characteristic of the practice (the typical and/or expected *relatings associated with, e.g., teaching, learning, health, or accountancy*), all oriented by the characteristic or distinctive kind of project they are practising.

Put simply, different occasions of practising require different practices, but these always involve mutually understood and configured sayings, doings, and relatings unique to practices of one kind or another. That is to say, sayings, doings, and relatings are coordinated or organised, yet also cohere around or 'hang together'

1.2 Practices

in the distinctive *project* of a practice (like learning a lesson, having a consultation with your doctor, or a meeting seeking financial advice), but at the same time are always temporally configured. Practices and practice architectures 'hang together' in what Schatzki (2002) describes as 'teleoaffective structures', and what Kemmis et al. (2014a, 2014b) called the *project* of a practice.

1.2.1 The Project of a Practice

When people are engaged in a practice, the *project* of a practice can be comprehended by their intuitive response to the question 'what are you doing?' (Kemmis et al., 2014b). Kemmis et al. (2014b, p. 155), described the project of a practice in this way; that it encompasses:

> (a) the intention (aim) that motivates the practice, (b) the actions (sayings, doings and relatings) undertaken in the conduct of the practice, and (c) the ends the actor aims to achieve through the practice (although it might turn out that these ends are not attained).

Thus, understanding practices means attending to ways the intricately interconnected and simultaneously produced sayings, doings and relatings 'hang together' in a project through *individual* (or subjective) and *intersubjective* achievements. It is in intersubjective spaces where:

(i) what people *say* and *think* (sayings) create a *semantic space* shared among interlocutors; it is made possible (or difficult or impossible) by the locally experienced conditions found in or brought to a site—that is, by the content and form of shared (or not shared) *language* and *specialist discourses* used.
(ii) what people *do* (doings) in the *physical space–time* is shared in activities with other embodied beings; it is made possible (or not) by locally experienced conditions where *actions, activities* and *work* get done amid the physical set-ups in the space and the material objects and resources that exist in the site; and
(iii) how people *relate* to others and the world (relatings) create the *social space* shared with other social–political beings who come together as interlocutors in interactions; it is made possible (or not) by locally experienced conditions influenced by the practitioner roles and relationships of *power, agency,* and *solidarity*.

These *intersubjective spaces* are where intersubjective meaning making exists, and form places and times where people encounter one another as interlocutors in practices, and together they engage, whether overtly or implicitly, in shared meaning making. These spaces include, for example, classrooms, meeting rooms, homes, sporting venues, and virtual environments.

An example: the project of a doctor consulting with a patient about their X-ray results.

Through its *sayings*, the consultation practice unfolds discursively in the site of practice—the doctor's surgery—using characteristic language (typical of the language used, for example English that is spoken and heard, thought, written and read) and discourses (typical of what is known and expected in a medicalised situation). The sayings of this consultation practice are, or become, understandable to those present (the doctor and the patient) as resembling a doctor–patient consultation (this is how the project of a consultation happens); whereby the doctor and the patient come together as interlocutors, and where intersubjective meaning making about the diagnosis and prognosis is the goal. As interlocutors they are interacting with one another to communicate their meanings and interpretations about what is happening in that consultation at that time—that is, they are creating an intersubjective space as their conversation unfolds. For example, in the case of consultation practices, the doctor and, increasingly, the patient, employ particular everyday and specialist medical terminologies and discourses about conditions, illnesses, treatments, and medicines to prescribe and treat the patient (e.g., specialist medical language like X-rays, anti-inflammatory medicines, prescriptions), and as they read particular medical journals or read and interpret the X-ray results from the radiologist—these form part of the sayings. The discourse here used is not merely something abstract or universal—since *as the consultation happened* in a particular place and time, it became site-specific for that particular patient and that particular doctor in relation to that particular circumstance. As the time passes, the language in which the practice of consulting is conducted, leaves behind specific memories, thoughts, practical knowledge, interpretations, and understandings about what happens in doctor-patient consultations. The site (the consultation in the particular surgery between a doctor and their patient) becomes a place for the use of this language (particular to 'explaining X-ray results' or discussing treatment options) to be interpreted and communicated by the those participating in the practice at the time—then and there.

Through its *doings*, the consultation practice engages people and objects in activities, activity-systems and work that are part of the material 'happening' of the physical site—in this instance, the doctor's surgery. For example, in the case of doctor–patient consultation, the doctor and their patient meet in a physical consulting room often in a setting furnished with material objects like the doctor's desk and patient chairs, an examination bed for patients, an overhead light, a computer for recording information, reading X-ray files and printing prescriptions; where particular resources (such as stethoscopes, syringes, bandaging equipment) are present and used when required, and which together enable the *activity* of consulting to be done. The activity of doing the practice of consulting with a patient about their X-ray results leaves behind different physical traces and consequences for both the doctor and the patient (in the form of completed patient records, referral letters, patient treatment plans, prescriptions, alleviation of pain, better health outcomes for the patient).

Through its *relatings*, the consultation practice connects people (e.g., the doctor, the receptionist, the practice nurse, the radiographer, and patient) and objects in varying roles and relationships that locate them as part of the site (albeit that some are not physically in the site at the time). For example, in the case of the doctor–patient consultation, the doctor exhibits a particular kind of authority (as a medical expert) with authoritative knowledge and brings this to the relationship with the more vulnerable less informed patient (tentatively engaging in the interactions since they are in pain, and varying feelings of hesitance depending on whether this is their regular doctor for example) as they encounter one another in the consultation on that day, where the doctor might advise or seek further specialised support, or the individual patient might exercise personal agency as they select/make decisions about their own treatment plan. The practice of consulting with a patient leaves behind traces in the relationships between the doctor, their patient and others, like their incumbency of particular roles (doctor, the patient, the specialist to whom the patient is referred, the radiographer who read the original X-rays on the peripheral), and specific ways of relating to others (medical team in solidarity with each other, the practice care nurse as responder to the doctor's directions), the connection to past doctor's visits or future treatments required by the patient, and increasing sense of agency as the patient becomes more informed or their condition improves.

As this example suggests, practices form parts of projects (e.g., the broader project of health care, or the general project of a doctor–patient consultation, or the specific project of explaining X-ray results). They simply do not happen devoid of internal or external influences that exist in or brought to the situation (circumstances, sites, and subjectivities); these influences reciprocally create enabling and constraining conditions of how the practice possibly unfolds in reality (influenced by who is present and their role in the practice, levels of familiarity with medical procedures and terminology, the in-the-moment interactions between the doctor and the patient, the prior interactions between the doctor and the radiographer and so on). These conditions are described as practice architectures and are outlined in the next section.

1.3 Practice Architectures

Practices do not merely appear in the place where they happen. Practices, formed by distinctive sayings, doings and relatings, are enmeshed within the places in which they take place. These, in intricately interconnected ways, create part of the way the practice 'gets done there and then' (of participating in a lesson in a classroom, a consultation in a doctor's surgery, or meeting with your accountant at his accountancy firm, for instance). In this way, a practice is a *nexus* (Schatzki, 2002) of sayings, doings, and relatings which happen—at the same time—and are bundled together amid existing *site-based* conditions and arrangements. These conditions are described by Kemmis et al. (2014b) as *practice architectures*. In their articulation of the theory of practice architectures, Kemmis et al. (2014b, p. 31) presented the view that:

> (a) individual and collective practice shapes and is shaped by (b) what we will describe as *practice architectures*, so that (c) the sayings, doings and relatings characteristic of the practice hang together in projects that in turn shape and are shaped by (d) practice traditions that encapsulate the history of the happenings of the practice, allow it to be reproduced, and act as a kind of collective 'memory' of the practice.

Here, practice architectures are the conditions that *influence*, shape, organise, and so arrange, how practices get done, where practice architectures are inextricably and resolutely linked with practices. Thus, practice architectures enable and constrain the sayings, doings, and relatings of practices, and so are formative and transformative of practices. The practice architectures that enable and constrain practices exist in three dimensions (semantic, physical space–time, and social) often, but not always, aligned with the activities of *saying, doing,* and *relating* and displayed as expressions in the media of language, work, and power. They constitute enabling and constraining preconditions for the conduct of practices, and appear in the form of:

- *cultural–discursive arrangements* (in the medium of *language* and in the dimension of *semantic space*) that are the resources that make possible the *language and discourses* used in and about this practice; these arrangements enable and constrain the *sayings* characteristic of the practice (e.g., constraining what it is relevant to say, or—especially—what language or specialist discourse is appropriate for describing, interpreting, and justifying the practice);
- *material–economic arrangements* (in the medium of *activity and work*, in the dimension of *physical space–time*) that are the resources that make possible the *activities* undertaken in the course of the practice; these arrangements enable and constrain the *doings* characteristic of the practice (e.g., by constraining what can be done amid the physical set-ups of various kinds of rooms and indoor and outdoor spaces in a school); and
- *social–political arrangements* (in the medium of *power and solidarity* and in the dimension of *social space*) that are the resources that make possible *the relationships between people and non-human objects* that occur in the practice; these arrangements enable and constrain the *relatings* of the practice (e.g., by the organisational functions, rules and roles in an organisation, or by the communicative requirements of the lifeworld processes of reaching shared understandings, practical agreements about what to do, and social solidarities) (Kemmis et al., 2014b, p. 32).

Practice architectures are 'bundled' together with practices in these three kinds of arrangements that enable and constrain possibilities for the shared sensemaking necessary for participating in social life (Edwards-Groves & Grootenboer, 2023; Weick, 1995). They form an inextricably linked mutually informing part of the 'living' distinctiveness of any particular site. The term 'living' is often used by proponents of the theory to reflect the dynamic realities of the nature of participating in practices, rather than more inert, static, or abstract representations. Understanding the particularity, distinctiveness, and happeningness of practices as they unfold in each site is critical. This means, in simple terms, that although the practices associated with lessons, consultations, or meetings (to use our rolling examples) happen every day in thousands of classrooms, surgeries, or accountancy firms across the world, no two lessons, consultations, or meetings are the same because the practice architectures in the different places are contingent on the different conditions present (at the particular time and in the particular place).

1.3.1 Making Sense of Practice Arrangement Bundles

The notion of practice arrangement bundles, represented as practices and practice architectures (i.e., the cultural–discursive, material–economic, and social–political arrangements) in the theory of practice architectures, can be understood in terms of the interrelatability between each component part of the dialectic. The use of the hyphen in the terms cultural–discursive, material–economic, and social–political, is a deliberate linguistic device to represent the inherent connections between each feature. Representing the different practice architectures in this way reflects the mutually informing reciprocal relationship between the individual concepts, showing how each side of the dialectic has equal bearing on the other. For example, as Schatzki (2012, p. 16) says 'the relationship between practices and material entities is so intimate, … the notion of a bundle of practices and material arrangements is fundamental to analysing human life'. The practice architecture dialectics form a critical conceptual foundation of the theory. These are discussed briefly next.

1.3.1.1 The Cultural–Discursive Dialectic

Connecting the cultural with the discursive reflects the interdependent relationship between culture and discursivity, since language and the symbols of language are cultural artefacts (for example, in spoken languages, or the English/Latin alphabetic system represented in texts, or Egyptian hieroglyphs, or the Chinese logo syllabic writing system consisting of logograms). As Kemmis et al. (2014b, p.2) say, 'participants in practices orient themselves and to one another through their *shared culture* by their *shared language* and symbols'. Language, discourses and cultural artefacts such as texts provide semantic structures for interacting and sensemaking where ideas might flow discursively through turn-by-turn interaction sequences produced and interpreted by interlocutors or represented abstractly in texts (oral, written, digital, etc.). As ideas pass discursively between interlocutors in their encounters (including conversations with varying degrees of formality), cultures are manifest in the language and discourses used (e.g., learning cultures are made apparent in the type of learning-oriented language discourses stakeholders use), and reciprocally, language and discourses create cultures. This idea takes as 'axiomatic the notion that culture as practice is inherently tied to language and discursivity—and its associated discourses, activities and interactions are living, dynamic and moving' (Edwards-Groves, 2023, p. 91), as so is treated as a verb rather than as a noun, which reflects overtones of culture as being fixed (after Brice Heath & Street, 2008).

1.3.1.2 The Material–Economic Dialectic

Connecting the material with the economic reflects the interdependency between spaces, materials, means, and ends. As Schatzki (2012, p. 16) says 'the relationship between practices and material entities is so intimate, … the notion of a bundle of practices and material arrangements is fundamental to analysing human life'. This means doing activities is inherently tied to materiality, and so intrinsically connected to the physical environment and material resources 'in play' that meaningfully contribute to the practices happening at the time. Spaces house resources, thus form and inform how structures (physical set-ups and objects) are used in practices, which at the same time, are inherently related to economics as means (so wealth, esteem and poverty, or privilege, disregard, and misfortune), and create the means to the ends through activity and production.

1.3.1.3 The Social–Political Dialectic

Connecting the social with the political reflects the interdependency between humans as social embodied beings and, as such, their relationships with others. Relationships are inherently tied to roles and thus tied to hierarchies of power, social solidarities, expressions of agency, or oppression. Thus, the social–political dialectic acknowledges the relational resources (in a site) that enable and constrain the relatings inherent in any unfolding practice.

1.4 Practicescapes: A Site Ontological, Historical, and Ecological Framing

Practices happen in the temporal flow of activity, where on each occasion of practising they unfold discursively through language amidst different relational configurations in sequences of real time (without interruption since time itself does not stop, thus they are themselves part of history-making action, Marx, 1852), and are or become *interwoven* (Kemmis et al., 2014b), *entangled* (Hodder, 2012), or *enmeshed* (Schatzki, 2002, 2010) with sites, not just 'set' in them. The site is a key focus for researchers using the theory of practice architectures as they seek to advance understandings about how diverse practices become *interwoven* in local sites, in what Kemmis et al. (2014b, p. 4) described, metaphorically, as *practice landscapes*. In this section we offer a brief outline of the influence of site ontological, historical, and ecological dimensions that, with practice architectures, comprise what we have rephrased as a **practicescape** (Edwards-Groves & Grootenboer, 2023). Since the focus of the theory of practice architectures is on practices and sites of practice, we use the word practicescapes in preference to the term practice landscape as a measure of conceptual precision. In our view, the term practicescapes sharpens the perspective, the '-scape', on the relationship between practices and sites, to the extent that practices in, and as, sites (after Schatzki, 2002) form an intricately interconnected part of the ***happeningness*** of practice.

The theory of practice architectures attends empirically to matters arising from three interrelated multifocal lenses—the historical, ecological, and site ontological features of a *practicescape*. As well, we have said elsewhere (Edwards-Groves & Grootenboer, 2023, p. xx),

> to understand how practices and practice architectures influence one another in sites, there is a need to see both the intricate minutiae of the moment-by-moment happenings in activity timespaces as well as understand the broader cultural, demographic, historical, economic and political conditions influencing the practicescape.

Key here is the interrelatedability between the broader conditions that influence practices. Three of these insights framing the theory of practice architectures are briefly described next, beginning with sections on historical and ecological influences, then followed by a more comprehensive discussion site ontological perspective presented.

1.4.1 Historical Framings

The practices of yesteryear, even yesterday, influence the practices of now. This idea relates to temporality, and how its across time focus is necessary for revealing the flow of influence of past practices on current practices. History prefigures, and so informs or shapes, practices as they adapt to changing times, participants, and local exigencies; that is, remnants from history create practice architectures that influence the sayings, doings and relatings encountered and produced in current occasions of practising. Accounting for the *historical* mean recognising practice traditions, and importantly questioning where ideas, activities or relational architectures come from. In brief, recognising the influence of history on practices, and why, how, and when they have happened to come to exist in sites, is helpful in understanding the conduct of practices, and ways different practice traditions carry forth. 'Retrieving a sense of [an] intellectual history is not an antiquarian pursuit' (Doecke et al., 2003, p. 100). Thus, directs the researcher to find empirical evidence of the circumstances of practices that are shaped by past discourses (so become cultural–discursive arrangements), past activities (so become material–economic arrangements), and past relational configurations (so become social–political arrangements) (Kemmis & Edwards-Groves, 2018). So, tracing the origins or the genesis of practices in terms of discourses, technical applications and methods, personal histories, and intellectual traditions that continue (to the present) to exert influence on the real-time enactment of practices provides the practice theorist with important insights for explaining what they are observing empirically (for example). Therefore, historicising practices matters (Hardy & Edwards-Groves, 2016), since practices come into existence in sites through evolutionary processes often emerging as practice traditions (Kemmis et al., 2014b) like education, health, business, politics.

1.4.2 Ecological Framings

An *ecological framing* allows researchers to understand the interrelatability between practices, and between practices and practice architectures (discussed in more detail in the next chapter). How practices in a complex of practices and practice architectures are inextricably related to and exert influence on one another form a key idea in the empirical study of practices. It stands to reason then, that the idea of an ecology of practices it not merely an abstraction. It represents the dynamic interrelationship between practices, and important for considering a site ontological perspective. Of interest is observing, in sites, the interconnections, interdependencies, and ecological relationships between the enabling and constraining conditions that reciprocally shape, and are shaped by, practices *and* practice architectures that are brought to bear on the moments of practising. That is, where some practices become practice architectures for other practices and vice versa. Although commonsensically, one might expect practices are connected in an abstract sense, the theory of practice architectures insists that practices themselves are observably ecologically connected, and thus form part of the empirical fabric of practice-based research.

1.4.3 Site Ontological Framings

The *site ontological* perspective[4] acknowledges distinctive local conditions and circumstances that influence the conduct of practices, enabling a view of the nuanced arrangements found at a site to be revealed (which also include historical influences, and happenings amidst an ecology of practices). This idea follows insights from Dewey (1933) and Freire (1985) for example, who suggest site ontological approaches provide authenticity to the view of practice being examined since it is interested in the particularity of how practices are happening then and there. Considering practice from the site outwards allows practices to be theorised as being relevant to particular sites where practitioners, in their practising, display or make visible the ethical, moral and affective dimension of their minute-by-minute day-to-day work (Grootenboer, 2018).

The site ontological nature of practice is one of the key features of the theory of practice architectures. This is a departure from a large body of work theorising practice, and thus its place in the theory forms a critical perspective to understand when interpreting practice and designing practice-based research. Put simply, it is

---

[4] This is discussion in more detail, and with particular reference to research study design, in Chap. 3.

about the *happeningness* of practices in activity time–space. Kemmis et al. (2014b, p. 33), reflecting on Schatzki's work, commented:

> Schatzki's theory [of practice] is an *ontological* theory of practices. It insists on the reality of practices as things that are always *situated* in time and space, and that unfold and happen in *site ontologies* (Schatzki 2005). While of course it addresses practices in general, Schatzki's theory requires us to understand that, as they occur in reality, practices are always located in particular sites and particular times. Practices are not performed from predetermined scripts; the way a practice unfolds or happens is always shaped by the conditions that pertain in a particular site at a particular time. The practices that we observe in real life are not abstractions with an ideal form of their own; they are composed *in* the site where they happen, and they are composed *of* resources found in or brought to the site: cultural-discursive resources, material economic resources, and social-political resources.

The primacy of the site is at the heart of the theory of practice architectures, and therefore, sees practices as being formed by the resources that exist, and are brought into, the place of the practice, as they unfold in real time–space. Yet, practice theorists are confronted with practice rhetoric often associated with policy initiatives bundled up as 'best practice' (for example) that sit counter to a site ontological view in that they treat practice as a unitary bounded package of 'best' solutions or approaches to a practice of one kind or another. Idealised notions of best practice sit glibly alongside a culture of performativity and mandates, neglecting the site-based needs and circumstances of particular people, in particular organisations, in particular communities. It is a 'political' line that neglects the constellation of practices that constitute a particular practice and the particular conditions that influence the conduct of practice as it is enacted in particular sites there and then (Edwards-Groves, 2018). As practice theorist Schatzki (1996, p. 2) writes, such a narrow view of practice,

> Treats the intricate and complex tangle of phenomena that constitutes social life as neatly tied up in a system and governed by systemic principles [and] neglects the contingent, shifting, and fragile relations among social phenomena that weave them into everchanging constellations. The point is not, at least usually, that these phenomena are autonomous and isolated, but instead that they constitute complex nexuses that do not add up to something beyond themselves.

Broadly, the theory of practice architectures is a theory that pushes beyond rhetorical understandings of practices by allowing us to 'get at' the density, porosity, and nuances of practical work as it happens in particular sites (Grootenboer et al., 2021). The premise here is simple, but the implications are not. As a primary concern, the site ontological feature of the theory of practice architectures specifies the central importance of view of practice that regards it, at once, as socially constituted (among people), dialogically formed (through language and communication), locally situated (in particular places) and as accomplished in real-time happenings (in a real-time flow). A site-based view deliberately accounts for the influence of the conditions present at a site on the practitioners and their accomplishment of practices.

The implications of this perspective are profound, not the least being that any notions of universal *best practice*, while widely lauded, need to be dismissed as fallacious and possibly harmful to improvement or development, and so transformation.

A site ontological perspective means that practices are not merely unfolding temporally in *sayings, doings,* and *relatings* in a particular context, but rather they are shaped—enabled and constrained, by the cultural–discursive, material–economic, and social–political resources that exist in a site at any particular moment in time and space. In this sense, practices and practice architectures are mutually constituting and inseparable from the site where they exist, and thus does not allow for a person-centric account to dominate the discussion.

To illustrate, imagine a teacher walking into a classroom full of students with a large bag of lollies (to be used as a resource in a sorting lesson in mathematics)—as soon as the teacher enters and the children see the big bag of candy, the site of teaching and learning, and thus the practice architectures that shaped the possibilities for learning and teaching, change. In this sense, the bag of sweets are not just part of the context—they have discursively, materially, and relationally altered the learning and teaching practice conditions, and practices that were possible before will now be altered to.

1.5 The Theory of Practice Architectures

Most commonly, the theory of practice architectures has been captured and represented by Fig. 1.1 that was first published in the seminal text *Changing Practices: Changing Education* (Kemmis et al., 2014b). We will use this visual representation to structure our discussion of the theory of practice architectures, but also point out some limitations and shortcomings that this figure can sometimes engender.

These aspects can be seen on the left-hand side of the figure, and this represents the 'side of the individual'. What is important to note here is that practices are *comprised* of sayings, doings, and relatings, not that practices *are* sayings, doings, and relatings—while each component might be identifiable and describable, they only have meaning as a whole—a practice. This is akin to saying that a sports team is comprised of forwards, backs, and midfielders—while each position can be seen and named, they only function in unison as a team. Importantly then, in using the theory to understand and critique practices, while there may be some value in noticing and labelling particular sayings, doings, and relatings, it is of little value if it not then considered vis-à-vis the practice as a whole.

On the right-hand side of the figure, the side of the social, are the *practice architectures* which are the characteristic conditions and arrangements that enable and constrain practices. More specifically, the sayings, doings, and relatings of a practice are enabled and constrained by particular *cultural–discursive, material–economic,* and *social–political* arrangements, that exist in the site of the practice.

1.5 The Theory of Practice Architectures

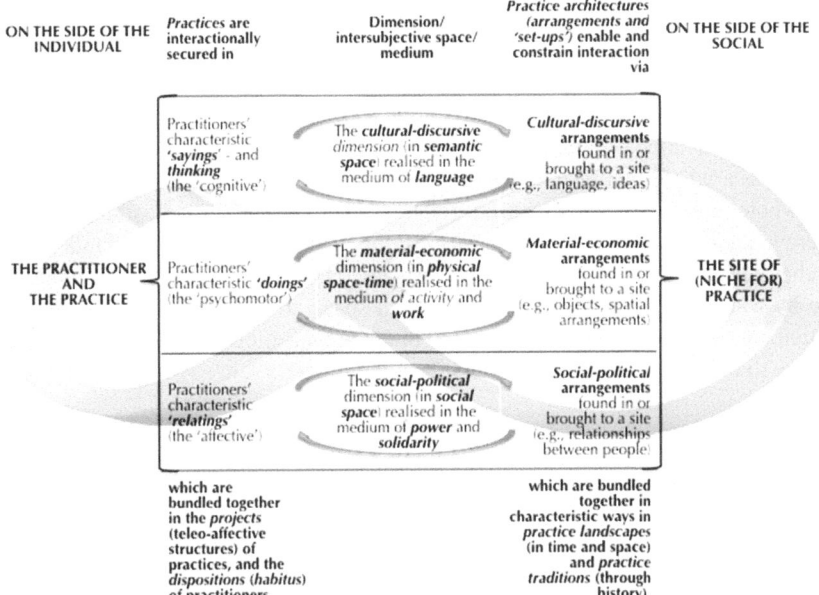

Fig. 1.1 Theory of practice architectures

1.5.1 Arrangements

The cultural–discursive arrangements and conditions are in, or brought into, a site and enable and constrain the sayings of the practice. To illustrate, the shared language of a group of people in a meeting will enable dialogue, but if there are some technical terms that are not widely understood, then the communication will be somewhat constrained, and the meeting practice limited. Similarly, the material–economic conditions found in, or brought to, a site enable and constrain the doings of a practice. For example, again considering the meeting practice, the material set-ups of furniture and equipment, and the arrangement of people in that space, will all impact and influence the nature and tone of dialogue that it possible. Third, the social–political arrangements found in a practice site will enable and constrain the relating in a practice. Again, considering the meeting practice, there are professional ethics and social norms that guide how individuals interact with one another in a meeting and these enable and constrain the relatings that characteristic the meeting practice in that particular site.

As with the 'sayings, doings, and relatings', the three arrangements forming the foundation of practice architectures can, to a degree, be identified, described, and named, but they do not operate in isolation—the cultural–discursive, material–economic, and social–political arrangements together form the practice architectures (in a site) and as a whole they enable and constrain practices. Relatedly, and importantly, while it is relatively easy to see the connection between sayings and cultural–discursive arrangements, doings and material–economic arrangements, and relatings and social–political arrangements, this is a simplification. Indeed, the above figure and often our descriptions (including those in the preceding paragraph) can be misleading because while the horizontal relationship is clear, it is the practice architectures as a whole that enable and constrain sayings, and the practice architectures as a whole that enable and constrain doings, and the practice architectures as a whole that enable and constrain relatings. To illustrate, in a business meeting where a client's financial plan is discussed, the way people present can talk to one another will be enabled and constrained by shared language and understandings, but also by where they are sitting in the physical space around the table, and how the participants at the meeting are positioned in the organisation's hierarchical structure relative to other partners, workers, and the client.

1.5.2 Interspatial Dimensions

The theory of practice architectures views practices within three dimensions of intersubjective space—where people, as interlocutors, encounter one another and the world in semantic, physical space–time, and social spaces. Accordingly, people come into these intersubjective spaces through their practices. Kemmis (2021, p. 4) explained the nature of these multidimensional spaces like this:

(1) semantic space, in which we encounter one another as interlocutors, in the medium of language, among the cultural–discursive arrangements found in or brought to a site (like the language we speak there, and the things we talk about there);
(2) physical space–time, in which we encounter one another and other things in the world as embodied beings, in the medium of activity and work, among the material–economic arrangements found in or brought to a site (like the familiar objects found there, and the times we spend there); and,
(3) social space, in which we encounter one another as social beings, in the medium of solidarity and power, among the social–political arrangements found in or brought to a site (like the changing and sometimes contested relationships we have with people there, in all their intersectionality in terms of things like race and gender and class and age and sexual orientation, for example).

1.5.3 An Example

To illustrate the theory of practice architectures, we now turn to an example of a practice—the practice of reading this book!

At the most rudimental level, the practice of reading this book involves you casting your eyes over the words and making sense of the text (sayings), while sitting in a comfortable chair holding the book and turning the pages (doings), while engaging with the ideas and us as authors (relatings). Your capacity to do this is enabled by your facility with English language, but perhaps constrained by some new terms, language or discourses (cultural–discursive arrangements); enabled by the paper or e-copy of the book you are reading, but maybe constrained by the time you have available to read (material–economic arrangements); and, the previous interactions you may, or may not, have had with some of the authors or previous texts read about the theory of practice architectures may enable and constrain how you read the ideas here (social–political arrangements).

Importantly with this example, where the practice may be unfolding in a solitary physical space, it can still be seen as social as we engage in the ideas about the theory of practice architectures through the pages of a book. Thus, the semantic space is bounded by the language we speak, and in this case with the particular nuances of academic writing and the specific related practice terms. The physical space–time is characterised by the book that you hold, and also the point in history when you are actually in dialogue with the ideas—reading the book now is a different practice than it would have been at another time, even though the actual book may be the same. Finally, the social space is charged by the social–political arrangements that are prominent for you as you read the text now. Your practice of reading this book will be different if you, for example, enter the space as a doctoral student or a tenured academic.

1.5.4 The Theory of Practice Architectures and Other Theories

In the foreword, where we briefly talked about the history of the development of the theory of practice architectures, we noted that we had been reading about praxis and other related topics, both as a group and individually, and we all had a deep understanding of some other philosophical schools of thought. Now you can see the theory, particularly as illustrated in Fig. 1.1, the threads of these other philosophical schools of thought and theories can perhaps be seen. For example:

- The 'sayings, doings and relatings' bear some resemblance to the philosophy of the ancient Greeks who looked to 'think well, act well, and relate well' or their domains of logic, physics, and ethics.
- The same three dimensions of practice have some synergy with Bloom et al.'s taxonomies—the cognitive, the psychomotor, and the affective domains.
- The three dimensions of the practice architectures reflect threads of Bourdieu's social fields and capitals—the cultural–discursive, material–economic, and social–political arrangements connect to the 'cultural and symbolic fields', 'economic field', and 'social field'.
- The mediums of the intersubjective space noted in the middle of the figure—language, activity and work, and power and solidarity, are Habermasian terms.

What this serves to show is that all new ideas and theories are not *brand new* per se, but rather built upon the ideas and writing from different intellectual and philosophical traditions of others. Obviously, the theory of practice architectures is no exception; and, in particular, if you are familiar with the writing of Schatzki, then you will see that this theory builds directly onto many aspects of his work.

1.6 Overcoming Practice Theory and Individual–Social Dualisms

Finally, and based on the sum of the previous discussion in this chapter, a feature of the theory of practice architectures is that its ontological nature allows apparent dualisms like practice and theory, and individual and social, to be considered interdependently. This can be valuable for analysing and understanding practices and their development because the theory of practice architectures offers a way 'to avoid or work without the common issues of dualisms like theory–practice and individual-social' (Choy et al., 2017, p. 268). Importantly, practices, practice architectures and practice sites are complex—and in fact the relationship between them is indissoluble. Thus, this theory provides productive and robust theoretical tools for researchers to acknowledge and investigate that complexity, avoiding unwelcome or unnecessary oversimplifications.

Additionally, the site ontological nature of the theory of practice architectures means that the happeningness of practices is the focus. In the case of teaching and learning, for example, the site

> ... a classroom in a school in its community, for example—is always the existential and ontological given in education. It is the place where things happen—where people meet and engage with one another in practice amid the practice architectures that make those practices possible. The site of a practice is the phenomenological reality that always and necessarily escapes standardisation in curricula, standards, assessments, and policies. The site is not only a matter of happenstance (where practices happen to take place and where things happen to be arranged as they are), nor only because the site is the specific location in which participants' practical deliberation and their practical action takes place. The 'site' is also crucial theoretically—to be understood in existential and ontological terms as an actual and particular place where things happen, not just as a location in an abstract and universal matrix of space-time. (Kemmis et al., 2014b, pp. 214–215)

This notion of the centrality of the site is important because, whatever theories or ideas people have, and however or why people create policies and develop particular conceptions, in the end, it is only in the practices that actually unfold in real time–space where insights about the efficacy, sustainability, and constraints become evident.

Importantly, the theory of practice architectures considers the individual and the social simultaneously and in a unified, integrated manner. This can be seen in the two mutually constituting sides of Fig. 1.1—it is not about practices *or* practice architectures; it is always about practices *and* practice architectures. So, for example, in considering leading practices in schools, there needs to consideration of the individual's integrated sayings, doings, and relatings, *and simultaneously* of the cultural–discursive, material–economic, and social–political conditions and arrangements that enable and constrain the leading practices (in that particular place). In this way, practices are not considered by an *either-or* premise—they are not understood as either an individual endeavour or a social phenomenon, but both (i.e., individual and social).

Finally, the theory of practice architectures (and other practice theories) draws the focus of inquiry and interest to the everyday and ordinary nature of practices—those aspects of life and professions that tend to be taken for granted. Nicolini (2012) said, 'the great promise of the practice lens is that of explaining social phenomena in a processual way without losing touch with the mundane nature of everyday life and the concrete and material nature of the activities with which we are all involved' (p. 9). In regard to education (to continue this rolling example), this focus on the *routine everydayness* of practice is important because, as Choy, Edwards-Groves and Grootenboer (2017, p. 268) argue:

> This is the 'bread and butter' of education—not the spectacular, one-off special lesson, or experience, but the normal ordinary unfolding of learning and teaching, and it is this dimension of education that demands attention simply because of its pervasiveness and commonality.

For us, our interest has always been in how practices can be viewed as the fabric of social life in all social fields (including as we have exemplified in education and educational practices; in health and health practices, in business and business practices, etc.). Regardless of the field or domain of interest, the same emphasis on 'grounding' practices in the situatedness and actual 'happeningness in time and space' can be centred and foregrounded.

1.6.1 The Challenge of a Site Ontological Practice Approach

From our experience, for many a practice site ontological perspective is difficult to grasp, perhaps because commonly in many fields of study, there is a default to an epistemological stance. Indeed, in many respects this is unavoidable because, even here, we are sharing *knowledge* about practice, but the point is to centre attention on knowing and understanding what happens—what is practiced, because this is what we all can experience. Furthermore, while we still need to apprehend practices as they unfold among local practice architectures, there is less of a *hermeneutical gap* than when we investigate beliefs or knowledge, because these things can only be accessed through some practice. For example, to try and appreciate if someone knows something, then we need to see them saying, doing, and relating things in certain ways, and from that we might infer that they have certain knowledge; whereas from a practice stance, the focus is on what actually happens with little need to make particular claims about what knowledge or beliefs or attitudes that it may infer—although it may be evident. This is a view that takes some time to grasp; and we will discuss this further in later chapters when focusing on conducting empirical studies using the theory of practice architectures, but for now we will provide this example related to educational leadership to illustrate.

Imagine that a trade college wants to understand how their leadership initiatives could yield higher educational outcomes for their students. On the one hand, they could take an *epistemological* approach that focuses on the leaders themselves, and undertake evaluative processes to determine their leaders' personality traits, and their beliefs and knowledge about education, leadership, and management. This might include a range of methods including quizzes, surveys, and even interviews, with the leaders and their teaching staff. From this data the college directors could then design professional learning for the leaders to help them grow in their knowledge of leadership, and how they can work with their personal qualities and strengths to achieve their goals. On the other hand, a *site ontological* approach could be to study for the leading practices that are evident at the college and take account of the associated practice architectures that enable and constrain the particular leading practices happening at the college. This might involve observing episodes and activities where leading is being practiced (e.g., a staff meeting), noting the sayings, doings, and relatings that are evident, and identifying any pertinent conditions and arrangements that are enabling and constraining these. To gain further insights, the leaders could be interviewed, and relevant policy documents could be reviewed, to uncover what discourses, activities, and relationships gave rise to their productive practices. This approach would provide a more comprehensive understanding of the leading as it happens in time and space in the college, and how it was possible under the local conditions that prevailed there. It then could be possible to look at the broader practice architectures—the conditions and arrangements that enable and constrain the leading, and understand how these can be changed and developed to allow different sorts of leading to flourish in ways that actually supported higher educational outcomes for their students.

1.7 Conclusion

This chapter has presented a detailed account of the foundation ideas and tenets of the theory of practice architectures. Many of the ideas introduced here may serve as a reference point for the material presented in the remainder of this book. A key idea to take to your reading of subsequent chapters is the inherent interelateablity between practices, practice architectures, and practicescapes; and thus, the site ontological nature of the theory of practice architectures. This key conceptual underpinning, in turn, raises the critical matter of focusing on the happeningness of practices unfolding in real time and space, the particularity of practices because of their situatedness and site-based conditions, and the interrelationship between practices. As the book progresses, we increasingly focus on undertaking research with the theory of practice architectures; but in the next chapter we discuss how practices are connected—the ecological relationship between practices.

References

Bourdieu, P. (1990). *The logic of practice* (trans: Nice, R.). Polity Press.
Bourdieu, P., & Wacquant, L. (1992). *An Invitation to Reflexive Sociology*. University of Chicago Press.
Brice Heath, S., & Street, B. (2008). *Ethnography: approaches to language and literacy research*. Teachers College Press.
Choy, S., Edwards-Groves, C., & Grootenboer, P. (2017). Provoking a (re)newed frontier in theorising educational practice. In P. Grootenboer, C. Edwards-Groves, & S. Choy. (Eds.), *Practice theory perspectives on pedagogy and education: Praxis, diversity and contestation* (pp. 265–280). Springer.
Corradi, G., Gherardi, S., & Verzelloni, L. (2010). Through the practice lens: Where is the bandwagon of practice-based studies heading? *Management Learning, 41*(3), 265–283.
Dewey, J. (1933). *How we think: A restatement of the relation of reflective thinking to the educative process*. D.C. Health & Company.
Doecke, B., Homer, D. & Nixon, H. (Eds.). (2003). *English teachers at work: Narratives, counter narratives, and arguments*. Wakefield Press.
Edwards-Groves, C. (2018). The Practice architectures of pedagogy: Conceptualising the convergences between sociality, dialogue, ontology and temporality in teaching practices. In O. B. Cavero & N. L. Calvet (Eds.), *New pedagogical challenges in the 21st century: Contributions of research in education* (pp. 119–139). InTech Publishing.
Edwards-Groves, C. (2023). Dialogic Pedagogies. *Oxford Handbook of Research in Education*. Oxford University Press.
Edwards-Groves, C., & Freebody, P. (2021). Literacy's changing morphologies: Trajectories, classroom exchanges and the evolution of literacy demands over the school years. *Australian Journal of Language and Literacy, 44*(2), 76–89.
Edwards-Groves, C. & Grootenboer, P. (2023). Practice architectures. *Oxford Handbook of Research in Education*. Oxford University Press.
Freire, P. (1985). *The politics of education: Culture, power and liberation*. Bergin and Garvey.
Garland, D. (2014). What is a "history of the present"? On Foucault's genealogies and their critical preconditions. *Punishment and Society, 16*, 365–384.
Green, B. (2009). Introduction. In B. Green (Ed.), *Understanding and researching professional practice* (pp. 1–18). Sense Publishers.
Grootenboer, P. (2018). *The practices of school middle leadership: Leading professional learning*. Springer.
Grootenboer, P., Edwards-Groves, C., & Kemmis, S. (2021). A curriculum of mathematical practices. *Pedagogy, Culture and Society*. https://doi.org/10.1080/14681366.2021.1937678
Hardy, I., & Edwards-Groves, C. (2016). Historicising teachers' learning: A case study of productive professional practice. *Teachers and Teaching: Theory and Practice, 22*(4), 538–552.
Hodder, I. (2012). *Entangled: An archaeology of the relationships between humans and things*. Wiley-Blackwell.
Hopwood, N. (2021). From response and adaptation to learning, agency and contribution: Making the theory of practice architectures dangerous. *Journal of Praxis in Higher Education, 3*(1), 78–94.
Ingold, T. (2011). *Being alive: Essays on movement, knowledge and description*. Routledge.
Kemmis, S. (2021). A practice theory perspective on learning: Beyond a 'standard' view. *Studies in Continuing Education*. https://doi.org/10.1080/0158037X.2021.1920384
Kemmis, S., & Edwards-Groves, C. (2018). *Understanding education: History, politics and practice*. Springer.
Kemmis, S., Edwards-Groves, C., Wilkinson, J., & Hardy, I. (2012). Ecologies of practices. In P. Hager, A. Lee & A. Reich (eds.), *Practice, learning and change* (pp. 33–49). Springer.

Kemmis, S., & Grootenboer, P. (2008). Situating praxis in practice: Practice architectures and the cultural, social and material conditions for practice. In S. Kemmis & T. J. Smith (Eds.), *Enabling praxis: Challenges for education* (pp. 37–62). Sense Publishers.

Kemmis, S., Heikkinen, H. L. T., Fransson, G., Aspfors, J., & Edwards-Groves, C. (2014a). Mentoring of new teachers as a contested practice: Supervision, support and collaborative self-development. *Teaching and Teacher Education, 43*, 154–164.

Kemmis, S., Wilkinson, J., Edwards-Groves, C., Hardy, I., Grootenboer, P., & Bristol, L. (2014b). *Changing practices, changing education.* Springer.

MacIntyre, A. (1981). *After virtue: A study in moral theory.* Duckworth.

Mahon, K., Francisco, S., & Kemmis, S. (Eds.). (2017). *Exploring education and professional practice—Through the lens of practice architectures.* Springer.

Marx, K. (1852/1999) The eighteenth Brumaire of Louis Napoleon. Marx/Engels Internet Archive. http://www.marxists.org/archive/marx/works/1852/18th-brumaire/ch01.htm Retrieved May 13, 2022.

Nicolini, D. (2012). *Practice theory, work, & organisation: An introduction.* Oxford University Press.

Reckwitz, A. (2002). Toward a theory of social practices. *European Journal of Social Theory, 5*(2), 243–263.

Schatzki, T. R. (1996). *Social practices: A Wittgensteinian approach to human activity and the social.* Cambridge University Press.

Schatzki, T. (2001). Introduction: Practice theory. In T.R. Schatzki, K. Knorr Cetina, & E. von Savigny (Eds.), *The Practice Turn in Contemporary Theory* (pp. 1–14). Routledge.

Schatzki, T. R. (2002). *The site of the social: A philosophical account of the constitution of social life and change.* Pennsylvania State University Press.

Schatzki, T.R. (2005). The sites of organizations. *Organization Studies, 26*(3), 465–484.

Schatzki, T. R. (2010). *The timespace of human activity: On performance, society, and history as indeterminate teleological events.* Lexington.

Schatzki, T. R. (2012). A primer on practices. In J. Higgs, R. Barnett, S. Billett, M. Hutchings, & F. Trede (Eds.), *Practice based education* (pp. 13–26). Sense Publishers.

Weick, K. (1995). *Sensemaking in organisations.* Sage.

Wenger, E. (1998). *Communities of practice: Learning, meaning and identity.* Cambridge University Press.

Chapter 2
Connecting Practices: The Theory of Ecologies of Practices

Abstract This chapter describes the characteristic interconnections between practices by specifically outlining the *theory of ecologies of practices* that accounts for how practices are ecologically arranged (in practice arrangement bundles) amid broader exigencies and locally encountered contingencies. This is an important conceptual resource that makes it possible to describe the inherent and varying kinds of interrelationships between practices and challenges practice-oriented researchers to account for these relationships in developing comprehensive understandings in any study of practices. We introduce the concept of *a practice complex* as being an integral to understanding the ranging, yet influential, meta-practices that indeed form practice architectures which shape how practices unfold amidst both broad and local conditions. Finally, we argue that the notion of a practice complex assists researchers and indeed practitioners of practices understand that practices are ecologically arranged, one that highlights the interplay between practices, practice architectures, and practicescapes. Drawing these ideas together we press for *site-based practice development* as an approach compatible with supporting a transformative agenda of change in different practice domains.

In the first chapter of this book, the focus was on practices and their associated practice architectures, and in doing so, introduced many of the conceptual resources fundamental to the theory of practice architectures. This chapter extends these concepts to account for the interrelatedness between practices by specifically outlining the *theory of ecologies of practices*, and what it means for researching practices. What has been shown clearly by many practice-based empirical studies is that in any practice site there are always multiple simultaneously unfolding practices, and importantly, that these practices do not occur independently of one another. Rather, much evidence illustrates that in any site there are many practices that, to a greater or lesser degree, are organised in ways that can be both described, observed and illustrated as arranged ecologically in relation to one another (Kemmis et al. 2012, 2014b). Appreciating the nature, and reach, of these ecological arrangements is important since when trying to understand how practices exist and come to exist in sites, attention must be given to the 'relational web' of practices (Grootenboer, 2018); these connections and interconnections are what make the phenomena of practices complex and multifaceted. To examine these ideas more fully, in this chapter we focus on the existential and site ontological interrelationships between practices.

As an introductory point, Kemmis et al. (2012) called the interdependence or interrelatedness between practices *an ecology of practices*. This concept allows the researcher to investigate the extent to which a particular 'species' or type of a practice is dependent on another practice. Therefore, when practices relate to one another in 'ecologies of practices' (Kemmis et al., 2012) within and across practices, they exist in relationships of interdependence. When practices are shown to be empirically interdependent, we see how different practices both shape and are shaped by one another. In reality, the 'outcomes' of one practice are 'inputs' to other practices (Edwards-Groves & Rönnerman, 2021) in the way that, for example, the practices of teaching and learning in classrooms can sometimes be dependent on one another, or how doctor–patient care is dependent on the national healthcare system, or in the way in which a particular practice of accountancy might be dependent on the economic practices legislated by a particular state. At a fundamental, even superficial level, the interdependencies are not hard to see. However, there are deeper and more nuanced features to how and why practices in a site are connected; this insight led the developers of the theory to describe practices as *ecologically arranged* (Kemmis & Edwards-Groves, 2018, Kemmis et al. 2012, 2014b). Grootenboer (2018, p. 52) put this idea succinctly:

> Practices do not exist and unfold in isolation—they exist and emerge in relation to other practices in the site. This means that practices are interdependent, interrelated and interconnected — they are ecologically arranged with other practices. In this way, ecologically connected practices in a given site will shape, and be shaped by, other practices.

Viewing practices as ecologically arranged denotes that the manner in which particular practices unfold in a particular site will symbiotically and interdependently sustain, or diminish, other practices within that practicescape. In this way, some practices can be 'hospitable' for other practices by creating 'niche' conditions and arrangements that enable them to occur in particular ways, and conversely, they can also be stifling of other practices, and constrain how they are able to happen. The ecological arrangements between practices in a site are conversely reciprocal in effect—in relation to what is enabled and constrained. For example, if a leader adopts more formal authoritarian-style leading practices, then the school decision-making practices are unlikely to be dialogic or democratic, but to the contrary, maybe these same decision-making practices might be expedient and quick—thus enabling some practices at the same time constraining others. As this example illustrates, the practices in a site are not independent—they are intimately ecologically related, with each enabling and constraining the others as they unfold in physical space–time.

Finally, before we proceed, just a note about the empirical examples predominately used in this chapter (and some of the other chapters)—our research has predominately been undertaken in educational sites and thus most of our illustrative cases are educational in focus and drawn from our own data sets. However, that said, we also use illustrative examples from health and business to exemplify the applicability and utility of the conceptual ideas we are explaining, knowing from other research undertaken around the world these theoretical resources have been usefully applied to understand practices, practicescapes, and ecologies of practices in a range of professionals, fields, and activities.

2.1 Ecologies of Practices as Related to Practice Architectures

Before describing the nature and implications of the ecological arrangement of practices in more detail, we first connect back to the relationship between these ideas and the theory of practice architectures. Put simply, the ecological relationships occur where one practice creates practice architectures for another practice. Indeed, the project of many practices (e.g., teaching, medicine, or accounting) is to overtly create practice architectures for other practices (e.g., learning, health, or financial viability). Practices and the practice architectures, or practice-arrangement bundles (after Schatzki, 2010), that support them, do not exist in isolation. Practices relate to one another in 'ecologies of practices' (Kemmis et al., 2012) within and across practices. When developing these theories from their seminal empirical study, Kemmis et al. (2014b, p. 43) commented:

> We have developed our theory of ecologies of practices in response to our observations of cases in which the *sayings, doings* and *relatings* that come into being as one practice unfolds become practice architectures that enable and constrain another practice. Thus, for example, the practice of teaching can become a practice architecture for the practice of student learning. In this case, the *sayings, doings* and *relatings* that constitute a particular practice of teaching become part of the practice architecture that supports the practice of learning; the teacher's sayings, doings and relatings become practice architectures for the students' learning. To put it more precisely, the specific *cultural-discursive, material-economic and social-political arrangements* that come into being and are materialised in the unfolding of a particular practice of teaching (teacher's sayings, doings and relatings) in a particular site enable and constrain the way the practice of learning can unfold for the students in the site.

Once considered, this is perhaps an obvious point. However, understanding the conceptual ramifications can have profound implications for researching practices, not the least being that practices prefigure other ecologically arranged practices, but they do not predetermine or preordain them. In their early writing, Kemmis and Grootenboer (2008) proposed that practices are held in place by 'preconditions' that includes the pre-existing cultural–discursive, material–economic, and social–political arrangements that enable and constrain some kinds of sayings, doings, and relatings, and so practices, at the expense of others. They used the term 'practice architectures' to describe these preconditions as site-based circumstances that prefigure practices and to make particular practices possible or not. Furthermore, there is always some degree of personal agency as people create, encounter, and participate

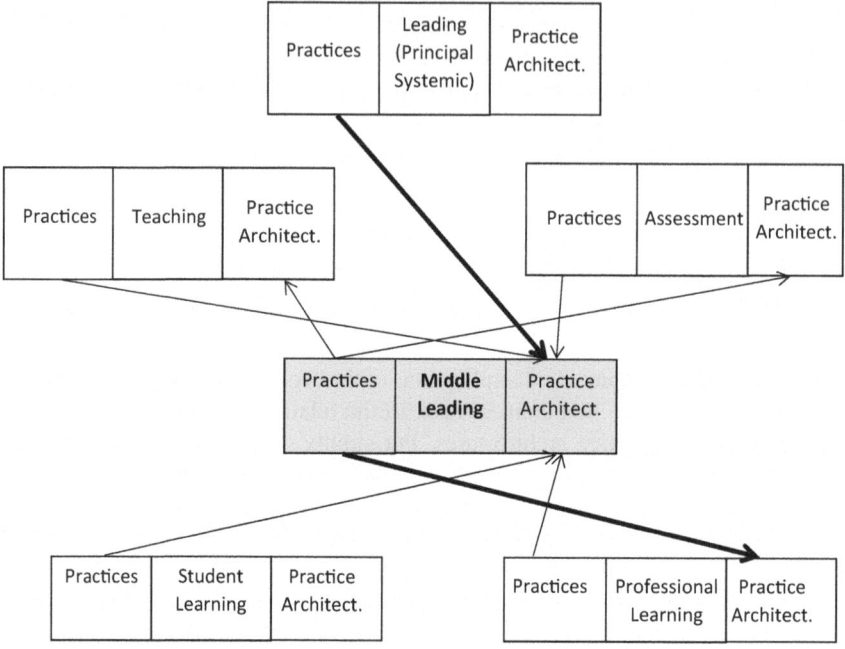

Fig. 2.1 Middle leading and the education complex of practices

in practices within the affordances and constraints created through the practices of others, albeit in some cases very limited.

In his book on educational middle leading practices, Grootenboer (2018, p. 138) tried to show these relationships diagrammatically (see Fig. 2.1).

Here, the relationships between the five meta-practices of the *Education Complex* (i.e., student learning, teaching, professional learning, leadership (system, principal and middle leading), and research, policy and assessment, discussed more fully later in this chapter) are shown using arrows. The connections between practices are empirically evident and indicate that certain practices provide the practice architectures for other practices, and that these relationships are usually reciprocal. To reflect these ecological relationships, proponents of the theory of practice architectures and ecologies of practices have used a variety of terms (including reciprocity, mutuality, inextricably linked, inherently connected, entwined, interdependent, interconnectedness, nested, entangled or enmeshed), to 'get at' the deep complex interelateablity between practices, practice architectures, and practicescapes.

2.2 The 'Ecological' Arrangement

The conceptual machinery comprising 'ecologies of practices' builds on Gherardi's (2009) metaphorical reference to the ecological relationship between human and non-human objects and Capra's (2005) biological theory. Drawing on Capra (2005), Kemmis and colleagues (2012) developed a theorised account of practical in-practice interrelationships to demonstrate how practices are interdependent (see, e.g., Kemmis et al., 2014b, pp. 45–54, for more detailed descriptions). The term 'ecological' is one that has been usefully drawn from the biological sciences, where it refers to the niche or 'ecology' where living things relate and interact with each other in mutually sustaining (or diminishing) systems. In employing the ecological concept, we are not claiming that practices are living things per se, but rather trying to emphasise the kind of inherent relationship between practices where in reality, they are always dynamic and in motion. With this in mind, the ecological principles of Capra (2005) have been variously applied in empirical research to help understand the ecological interdependent relationship between practices. These principles, as they are proposed in the theory of ecologies of practices, are represented in Table 2.1.

The ecologies of practices perspective offers researchers a way to capture the taken-for-granted complexities and interdependent natures of practices and has the potential to provide new insights into the more expansive range of constituent practices that happen in a range of practice domains (Edwards-Groves & Rönnerman, 2013). As the examples above show, these ecological principles are useful in understanding practicescapes and aid comprehension of the complex relational web of practices in any given site.

2.2.1 Ecological Interdependencies

Some of these principles are somewhat self-evident, as, for example, it is clear that many practices exist in a *network* of practices. For example, student assessment practices are only relevant and useful because they are nested within teaching and student learning practices, where assessment is related to what has been taught and learned, and in turn, assessment informs teaching practice. The principle of *nested systems* is evident in practice sites because it can be seen that practices exist in layers and levels where certain ones can be seen as nestled within 'larger' or more 'overarching' practices. For example, the practice of learning letters and words is nested in a broader practice of learning to read, which is nested in a broader practice again of reading to learn, and so it could go on; for a medical doctor, the practice of examining a child's throat is couched within a practice of diagnosing illness. Furthermore, these nested levels of practice are networked, meaning the practices at a particular layer partly create the practice architectures—the conditions and arrangements, for the practices at the other levels. Finally, the relevant practice architectures will be those that exist for any given practice at their 'layer' in the nested system. For example, educational

Table 2.1 Ecological principles of practices

Ecological principles	If practices are living things and ecologies of practices are living systems, then …
Networks	Practices derive their essential properties and their existence from their relationships with other practices—*for example, when participants in a course are organised into groups that regularly meet over a period of time with a facilitator, interdependent networks of practices emerge, including networks of facilitators of professional development, of classroom teachers, of specialist teachers*
Nested systems	Different levels and networks of practice are nested within one another—*for example, practices of teaching, professional learning and teacher leading exist and develop as interconnected practices connected to one another in nested systems*
Interdependence	Practices are dependent on one another in ecology of practices, as are ecologies of practices—*for example, participating in longer-term professional learning programmes is generative of both teacher development, student learning and teacher leading practices*
Diversity	An ecology of practices includes many different practices with overlapping ecological functions that can partially replace one another—*for example, teachers (and their student and school communities) are diverse, and so too are their specific development needs, additionally the professional learning and leading practices are not only different practices but are dependent upon one another and dependent upon their relationships with the processes and practices of particular professional development programmes, the different school and different system practices*
Cycles	Some (particular) kinds of matter (or in education—practice architectures, activities, orders or arrangements) cycle through practices or ecologies of practices like in a food chain—*for example, a curriculum cycle, a teaching and learning cycle*
Flows	Energy flows through an ecology of practices and the practices within it, being transformed from one kind of energy to another (in the way that solar energy is converted into chemical energy by photosynthesis) and eventually being dissipated—*for example, knowledge of how to teach reading, flows from the professional development program to the teacher, to the teaching practice to the student's learning to read*
Development	Practices and ecologies of practices develop through stages, adapting over time to the site-based conditions—*for example, professional learning practices strengthen the development of teaching practices, and over time have the potential to develop and strengthen leading practices, where teacher leaders develop through enactment (doing), evolving (doing with variations and contextual accommodations) and transforming (doing practices differently as their own)*
Dynamic balance	An ecology of practices regulates itself through processes of self-organisation, and (up to breaking point) maintains its continuity in relation to internal and outside pressures—*for example, teachers facilitating professional learning required both the internal (such as their desires) and external (such as time for meetings, support from a principal) conditions to exist in a dynamic balance, with each strengthening the conditions for the existence, development and sustainability of the other*

Adapted from Edwards-Groves and Rönnerman (2013, pp. 127, 137)

2.2 The 'Ecological' Arrangement

leading practices occur in school departments or teams, at the level of the principal, in system offices, and at high government levels. As you move through each 'layer' of the nested leading practices, the conditions and arrangements that enable and constrain those practices are different and site based—the site at the government level is broad and quite general, and at a large distance from the classroom, whereas the curriculum leader in a school team will be in a site that is much more locally and specifically defined because their 'level' is closer to the core site of education—classrooms. Similarly, the practices of setting health care policies and arrangements for the state's Chief Medical Officer provides broad and general conditions under which a local doctor in their own practice can provide medical care for particular patients at particular times. This means that, among other things, to understand and develop practices there is a need to apprehend how the said practice is ecologically nested within other relevant practices.

What is probably clear from the preceding discussion is that practices are *interdependent* in any given site, and this means that practices are maintained, or decreased, by other practices with which they are ecologically arranged. Thus, for example, in a doctor's surgery—a particular practice site, the health practices of their patients would be related to the doctor's examining, diagnosing, and prescribing practices; and in a classroom, one would hope and expect that students' learning practices are ecologically interdependent with the teachers' pedagogical practices. And of course, the converse would also be the case, where the doctor's or the teacher's practices were respectively impacted by the patient's or student's related practices. For instance, if a doctor used more 'natural' remedies and practices, then maybe the patients might respond with related personal health practices, and perhaps, have less reliance on formally prescribed medicines or traditional medical interventions practices. Similarly, if a teacher employed open-ended group-based tasks, learning practices that involved dialogue, inquiry and investigation might be encouraged and sustained, but perhaps rote practices and memorisation might be diminished. And, of course, if the students do not engage in the open-ended tasks and resist talking about their learning, then the associated teaching practices might be seen as less viable, and so consequentially, here, the student's learning practices shape teaching practices.

In terms of *diversity*, it is rather obvious that in any given site, there are a range of different practices and practitioners of practices that are ecologically connected. At a rudimentary level, then, drawing on the examples above, there is a need for teaching practices and learning practices—it would be a frivolous exercise for a teacher to engage in their pedagogical practices if there were no student learning practices occurring. Similarly, there would be no point in a medical doctor engaging in diagnostic practices if the patients were unable to unwilling to actually take up the prescribed health practices. Of course, in any of these practicescapes, there are many diverse practices involved (e.g., drug development, medical research, assessment and evaluation practices, training and leading practices), and at a range of organisational levels.

According to Capra (2005), in an ecosystem 'matter cycles continually through the web of life' (p. 25), and while this may be a little harder to see in practices, there is a sense that practices move through in predictable, systematic, and cyclical ways both within the layers or in spirals that move to other levels of particular practice landscapes. In a simple example, the teaching and learning cycle in classroom teaching design operates on the idea that teachers of a particular grade level firstly find out about their students' learning needs; once this information is gathered by a diverse range of assessment practices and procedures, the teacher designs or programmes their lessons based on what the students in the class need to learn next and what the curriculum advises them to teach; they then teach; this process then cycles back to finding out what the students now have learnt by assessing them once again, before moving on to the next unit. These cycles of teaching and learning happen systematically and predictably across the year school until the cohort moves to the year grade level, where the cycle of practices continues again.

The notion of *flow* refers to the movement of energy across and through 'the ecology of practices and the practices within it' (Kemmis et al., 2014b, p. 49), where one practice would provide the 'energy' or impetus that enables other practices in any given site. This energy flows because one practice creates conditions and arrangements that are conducive, hospitable, and supportive of other practices. This might occur, for example, by educational leading practices that provide cultural–discursive resources (e.g., policy directions, school values), material–economic arrangements (e.g., time, funds, space), and social–political conditions (e.g., encouragement), that provide 'energy' for pedagogical development. In this way the 'energy' flows from the leading practices through to the staff development practices, which hopefully, in turn, will flow to teaching practices and then student learning practices. Perhaps this is also evident in medical practices where, for example, nurses provide a sense of human care and understanding, and while patients try to comprehend some perhaps, difficult diagnoses, the nurses caring 'energy' flows from their nursing practices to the patient's health practices.

In recent years there has been discussion about *learning* being integral to practices (Grootenboer & Edwards-Groves, 2019; Kemmis et al., 2017)—when engaged in a practice it involves 'learning how to go on in the practice' (Grootenboer et al., 2021). Thus, *development* is part of practising, and this is the case for all practices. In this sense, learning is not so much a separate practice, but rather it is simply an integral part of practicing; for instance, as one engages in a practice of say diagnosing, then one is also learning about diagnosing, whether as a neophyte medical practitioner or as an experienced surgeon. This relates directly to Capra's seventh principle of an ecosystem, 'All living systems develop, and all development invokes learning' (Kemmis et al., 2014b, p. 27). This consistent development of practices and ecologies of practices, as they grow and build on previous development, means that forms of practices (and ecologies of practices) are always superseding previous versions. Of course, this development is essential for practices to thrive and survive as the site constantly changes and evolves; and conversely, if the practice architectures are such that growth is stifled, then the associated practices will diminish.

Finally, Capra (2005) posited that ecosystems exist in *dynamic balance* where the 'ecological community continually regulates and organises itself' (Kemmis et al., 2014b, p. 28). This dynamic balance is evident in sites where several practices unfold simultaneously in a concerted manner, with each practice creating the practice architectures, at least partially, for the others. In this way, the functioning and development of an ecology of practices is dependent on them unfolding in mutually affirming ways. Thus, while we often talk about certain practices, in terms of education, or health/medicine or business, the dynamic balance and interdependence between and within practices necessitates that it is more appropriate to consider them as ecologies of practices.

While we have discussed the principles of an ecosystem in a largely separated way, it is important to note that 'the purpose of these ecological principles is not that they are meaningful and useful individually, but rather as a coherent set or group (i.e., ecological principles are themselves ecological)' (Grootenboer, 2018, p. 141). In other words, it is not just that practices might be in dynamic balance or interdependent, but rather that, to a greater or lesser degree, all the principles apply in an interrelated interdependent manner. Furthermore, as was noted previously, Capra's (2005) principals were about living systems—not practices per se, but nevertheless they provide some important figurative insights about how, in any practice site, the practices that enter or exist there are related with ecological properties.

2.3 A 'Practice Complex'

In this section, we propose that practices in any field or domain appear as part of a complex of interrelated ecologically connected practices, we describe as a *Practice Complex*. In using the term 'complex' as we have here, first, acknowledges the complexity of the relationships between the range of broadly overarching or meta-practices. Second, that since practices are inextricably connected, they are somewhat pragmatically meaningless to be understood in isolation—thus, they need to be studied and understood in their complexity. Third, and relatedly, the term refers to the notion of a 'complex' as in how it is used to describe a particular site (e.g., like the architecture of an apartment complex where although the different apartments are separated by walls and floors, they are also connected by corridors, elevators, electricity connections). While our running examples to date have included education, health, and business, in this section we turn to a specific *practice ecology* related to education and schooling to exemplify this concept. If you are engaged in the education sector, then this will have some familiarity to you, but for those who are coming to these theoretical ideas from another field, then perhaps you can consider what the 'meta-practices' might be for you, and how they might form their own particular 'complex'. Also, in light of the preceding discussion about the nested nature of ecologies of practices, it is clear that while these are always experienced and understood locally, meta-practices are evident more broadly at the outer levels of the nested relationships.

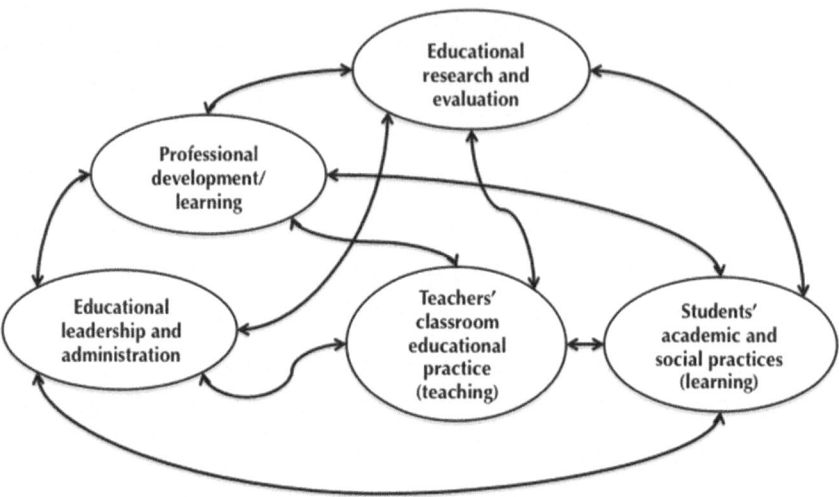

Fig. 2.2 Education complex

2.3.1 The Education Complex of Practices

At the time of introducing the theory of ecologies of practices, Kemmis et al. (2012) discussed explicitly the five *meta-practices* of education that have been evident since the inception of formal compulsory mass schooling. It has typically been represented by the diagram shown in Fig. 2.2 which was first published in the seminal book 'Changing Practices, Changing Education, although it was erroneously titled 'the theory of ecologies of practices' at the time.

As will be clear from some of the ideas presented in the previous section, the theory of ecologies of practices is much broader than these five particular practices, and so this particular idea and diagram has been called the 'Education Complex of Practices' (or generally just referred to as the Education Complex). Put simply, the contention is that the five education meta-practices are ecologically arranged and have always been evident as being interrelated throughout the history of compulsory schooling; these are:

- teaching;
- student learning;
- teacher education and professional development;
- educational leadership; and
- educational research and evaluation.

Once contemporary mass schooling emerged as a consequence of the industrial revolution (in the 1730s), these five kinds of practices began to be regarded as mutually necessary within a single, coordinated project of education. Student learning was thought to depend on teaching; teaching was thought to depend on the initial and

2.3 A 'Practice Complex'

continuing professional development and professional learning of teachers; schools and school systems needed to be regulated by educational policy, research and administration and by various kinds of practices of leading (such as systemic, principal and middle leadership). In line with broad state policies, these practices needed to be brought under control by a watchful eye of government, and this informed and developed modern conceptions of research and evaluation—so each could be improved in its connections with the others. The connections between these practices arose rapidly and simultaneously with the advent of mass schooling (Kemmis et al., 2014b, p. 51). While these practices have taken different forms and unfolded in particular ways in particular nation states over extended periods of time, their enduring presence clearly shows how their ecological arrangement has seen them develop and be sustained in ways which form practice traditions.

The ideas of a *Practice Complex* have particular implications for researching, understanding, and enacting and developing practices in different fields or domains, in studying how education it is rolled out in schools, or how health care is provided in hospitals or surgeries, or how business is conducted in accountancy firms. In the case of education, at the most fundamental level, there is an imperative in any educational development agenda to simultaneously consider all five of the practices in the Education Complex—their intimate and enduring ecological arrangement means that to make change and see growth, then change will need to be made in all five practices. This is not to say that attention and focus cannot be given to a particular practice, but any development will not be sustainable (due to their interdependence) unless allied attention is given to the other practices. Furthermore, because meta-practices exist in robust ecological networks regardless of fields or domains of study, it is not just that they have to be considered in turn, but rather, they need to be attended to as an interrelated complex whole. These insights also show how a practice is more than the sum of its parts.

Drawing this together, Grootenboer (2018, p. 54) explained this in this way:

> So, what this means is that to change practices there will also need to be associated changes in the practice architectures that enable and constrain these practices, and secure them in place, and it also requires a change in the practices that are ecologically connected to the practices concerned. For example, and specifically here, changing particular practices of middle leading will entail also changing the associated practices of professional development, teaching, learning and evaluation that are part of the ecology of practices in the particular site.

To illustrate, if a school community was concerned about rising incidents of bullying at the school, there might be a decision of the leaders to implement an 'anti-bullying' initiative. As part of the initiative, a classroom programme is developed, but to achieve this, the leading practices need to enable the required staff development practices by providing time, resources, support, and policies. Through their professional learning practices, teachers can enact new teaching practices that facilitate student learning practices vis-à-vis appropriate ways to behave towards others. To ascertain whether the initiative is being successful in curtailing bullying, research and evaluation practices could be developed and implemented, and these in turn could enable and constrain the further development of the initiative. Of course, it could also be appropriate to involve the practices of a range of others including community members and student leadership bodies.

This brief example illustrates in a very general and simplistic manner how the practices of the Education Complex are ecologically arranged. But we also note that while this unspecific illustration might provide a general approach or policy guideline about ways to go about addressing the issue; in some respects, it defies the very specific site-based nature of practices and how in reality, they actually unfold in particular places at particular times amidst particular conditions. Nevertheless, it does illustrate how, for example, how notions of a Practice Complex (or Complex of Practices) can be usually employed to consider ways practices as happening in site-specific ways (regardless of domain and settings like in schools, hospitals, or businesses).

2.3.2 The Implications for Research

It is reasonable to see how the theory of ecologies of practices and the Practice Complex offer conceptual resources, or even research tools, that can be employed to describe, and frame, what is happening in a range of practice sites. However, just to be clear, these are not just generalised abstract notions that, for example, teaching influences learning or nursing influences improved health outcomes, but rather, practices within a site are intimately interrelated in mutually sustaining ways as each practice creates the practice architectures for other practices. Thus, the focus should not be on the practitioners per se—the teachers, leaders or students, or doctors, nurses, or patients; but rather on their practices (here teaching, leading or learning practices, or consulting, nursing or patient practices), *as* they unfold in real time and space. To exemplify, Kemmis et al. (2014b, p. 44) commented:

> We are not so much interested in saying that, *in general*, practices and practice architectures of *professional learning* shape practices and practice architectures of *teaching*, for example, as in showing how *in practice*, the particular practices and practice architectures of one practice come to shape or be shaped by the practices and practice architectures of another practice.

While the capacity to describe and even understand the separate facets of practices is probably quite useful, in our mind it misses the key importance of these theories—that is, they (including the theory of practice architectures) are *critical* theories (Kemmis, 2019). They are powerful frames for showing how, when, why, and where, practice development in the wide range of diverse fields may not be sustainable or possible, unjust, and discriminatory, and irrational. Here specifically, understanding the notion of a Practice Complex has important implications for researching practices, since, as we argue, taking a narrower approach to understanding and developing practices in the different domains of study (education, health, or business to use our field examples) is ineffective, even futile—restricting potential research impacts and benefits of development activities. As such, to comprehend and develop

2.3 A 'Practice Complex'

practices, the more comprehensive multifaceted nature of practices as they are set in their varying Practice Complexes needs to be understood and changed in terms of their multifacetedness, complexity, and situatedness (discussed in the next chapter), where researchers, policy-makers, and practitioners are all equally considerate of various complexes of interrelated practices in the different domains. This approach considers, more widely and authentically, the conditions and arrangements in the particular practice domains, and so results can be more responsive in their consideration to particular sites. Therefore, we argue that any agenda for transformation must account for, and be customised towards, approaches that valorise site-based practice development (akin to the notion of site based education development we use in our own field of research) the within and beyond the relevant Practice Complex.

A key reason for this sentiment is that all too often we have seen government agencies or other bureaucracies trying to lead or implement reform initiatives (in education, healthcare or business) by, for example, providing or mandating new policies, legislation, change agendas or protocols (in the forms new curricula, development initiatives, information websites, laws, and so on). Yet, their impact is restrictive since they simply fail to provide adequate access to all, or to overtly take notice of the distinctive site-based conditions influencing different demographics or geographical locations where the initiative of the policy is to reach, or consider seriously the range of site-based conditions and arrangements appropriate for the necessary associated practitioner development to take place in particular places, or limitations are placed on the favoured mechanisms for change. So, as a consequence, practices are not reformed at all or that changed practices largely remain unsustainable because of the lack of attention to the complex of practices happen in each site. For example, if educational development is to be achieved, then attention needs to be given equally to each facet of the Education Complex of Practices in ways that address leading practices, staff development practices, teaching practices, learning practices, and assessment and evaluation practices, and this needs to occur at a local site level. Or, if improved health care is to be achieved, then attention needs to be given equally to each facet of the Complex of Health Practices in ways that address hospital leading and management practices, ongoing nurse education practices, nursing practices, patient care and administration practices, and this needs to occur at the local hospital site.

For researchers, the challenge here is to appreciate how to broaden the gaze in terms of the ecology of practices related to the key area of focus. In any given practicescape, there will be many practices that are ecologically arranged in a web of mutually sustaining relationships. Some of these will be obvious and closely connected, like in a school setting the five meta-practices of the Education Complex are always evident and influential; but there are also other practices present at the site—for example, the cleaning practices that ensure that the facilities are ready for students and teachers or the communication practices between the school and the parents to ensure information sharing necessary for educating. These kinds of peripheral practices do, but to a lesser extent, have an impact on the cultural–discursive, material–economic, and social–political arrangements of teaching and learning practices in the school, and thus perhaps might not warrant as much attention in the investigation of educational practices in a school. However, nonetheless, decisions about which practices to include in a study at a particular site cannot be considered arbitrary in the sense that they are all ecologically related in mutually sustaining ways, and perhaps it is wise to determine the limitations as they become apparent in the empirical work.

We acknowledge that this section has been largely focused on educational practices, and specifically the education complex. While we are aware of research that draws on, and tests the applicability of these concepts and theoretical ideas (particularly the notion of a *Practice Complex* akin to the education complex, or that of *site-based practice development* akin to site-based education development) in different practice domains (e.g., health, business, and agriculture), we wanted to present ideas and concepts that have been deeply grounded in our own empirical research work—not just ideas that we constructed to illustrate key points (although we have done this to a degree since we are not health or economics researchers). For us, the integrity of the development of these conceptual ideas is paramount, so presenting actual findings and theoretical tools that arose from real empirical research practices undertaken at a particular time and in particular places, has been key for the validity and reliability of the theoretical propositions we are making.

2.4 Conclusions

This chapter has presented important theoretical and conceptual ideas that accompany research applying the theory of practice architectures. Specifically, we described the *ecologies of practices* in relation to how practices are ecologically arranged (in practice arrangement bundles) amid broader exigencies and locally encountered contingencies. We illustrated this idea in terms of Capra's ecological principles that describe the inherent and varying kinds of interrelationships between practices, and argued for practice-oriented researchers to account for these relationships in developing comprehensive understandings in their study of practices. We introduced the concept of *a practice complex* as being an integral to understanding the ranging, yet influential, meta-practices that indeed form practice architectures which shape how practices unfold amidst both broad and local conditions. Finally, we argued that the notion of a practice complex assists researchers and indeed practitioners of practices understand practices as ecologically arranged, one that highlights the interplay between the practices, practice architectures, and practicescapes. Drawing these ideas together we pressed for *site based practice development* as an approach compatible with supporting a transformative agenda of change in different practice domains.

In the first two chapters of this book (that includes this one), we have intentionally laid the theoretical foundations for researching practices using the theory of practice architectures and the theory of ecologies of practices. As noted, these theories arose over an extended period of time while we simultaneously engaged with empirical research projects and immersed in the related theoretical and philosophical literature.

Of course, the development of the theories was itself a practice, or perhaps more accurately an ecology of practices, and so as such, these ideas were shaped by the prevailing practice architectures in that particular practicescape (we were engaged in) at that time and in that place. And, because of the developmental nature of the theory development, it also means that the conceptual ideas emerging from the early work are equally open to development as other researchers, in other places and at other times, engage with the theories and use the ideas, in new sites.

In the three chapters that follow, we turn our focus towards researching practices with the theory of practice architectures. In particular, we consider the situatedness of practices by looking at how one might design a study, and its relevant methodology, that seeks to understand practices of interest to the researcher, and the types of empirical data that might be collected to support a practice-based study. We then draw attention to data analysis, and some of the kinds of analytic methods that can be used to organise and interpret practices. Finally, we consider ways research findings can be communicated effectively as part of a strategic dissemination strategy, and thus reported in meaningful far-reaching ways that are consistent with a site ontological foundation.

References

Capra, F. (2005). Speaking nature's language: Principles for sustainability. In M. K. Stone & Z. Barlow (Eds.), *Ecological literacy: Educating our children for a sustainable world* (pp. 18–29). Sierra Book Club Books.

Edwards-Groves, C., & Rönnerman, K. (2013). Generating leading practices through professional learning. *Professional Development in Education, 39*(1), 122–140.

Edwards-Groves, C., & Rönnerman, K. (2021). *Generative leadership: Rescripting the promise of action research.* Springer.

Gherardi, S. (2009). Introduction: The critical power of the 'practice lens.' *Management Learning, 40*(2), 115–128.

Grootenboer, P. (2018). *The practices of school middle leadership: Leading professional learning.* Springer.

Grootenboer, P., & Edwards-Groves, C. (2019). Learning mathematics as being stirred into mathematical practices: An alternative perspective on identity formation. *ZDM Mathematics Education, 51*, 433–444.

Grootenboer, P., Edwards-Groves, C., & Kemmis, S. (2021). A curriculum of mathematical practices. *Pedagogy, Culture and Society.* https://doi.org/10.1080/14681366.2021.1937678

Kemmis, S. (2019). *A practice sensibility: An invitation to the theory of practice architectures.* Springer.

Kemmis, S., & Edwards-Groves, C. (2018). *Understanding education: History, politics and practice.* Springer.

Kemmis, S., Edwards-Groves, C., Lloyd, A., Grootenboer, P., Hardy, I., & Wilkinson, J. (2017). Learning as being 'stirred in' to practices. In P. Grootenboer, C. Edwards-Groves, & S. Choy. (Eds.), *Practice theory perspectives on pedagogy and education: Praxis, diversity and contestation* (pp. 45–65). Springer.

Kemmis, S., Edwards-Groves, C., Wilkinson, J., & Hardy, I. (2012). Ecologies of practices. In P. Hager, A. Lee, & A. Reich (Eds.), *Practice, learning and change* (pp. 33–49). Springer.

Kemmis, S., & Grootenboer, P. (2008). Situating praxis in practice: Practice architectures and the cultural, social and material conditions for practice. In S. Kemmis & T. J. Smith (Eds.), *Enabling praxis: Challenges for education* (pp. 37–62). Sense Publishers.

Kemmis, S., Heikkinen, H., Fransson, S., Aspfors, J., & Edwards-Groves, C. (2014a). Mentoring of new teachers as a contested practice: Supervision, support and collaborative self-development. *Teaching and Teacher Education, 43*, 154–164.

Kemmis, S., Wilkinson, J., Edwards-Groves, C., Hardy, I., Grootenboer, P., & Bristol, L. (2014b). *Changing practices, changing education.* Springer Education.

Schatzki, T. R. (2010). *The timespace of human activity: On performance, society, and history as indeterminate teleological events.* Lexington.

Chapter 3
Situating Practices: A Site Ontological Perspective to Study Design

Abstract In this chapter, we expand on ideas about the critical importance of understanding and accounting for the locally situatedness, and so *site ontological* nature, of practices as a key foundation of the theory of practice architectures. According to the theory, understanding the nature of practices demands attention to the realities of the kind of nuanced site-contingent activity accomplished by practitioners of practices. Specifically, the chapter describes how understanding the in-situ nature of how practices are occasioned in particular places and at particular times provides theoretical grounds for highlighting how practices are socially constituted (among people), dialogically formed (through language and communication), as ecologically interrelated (with other practices), and as accomplished in real-time happenings (in a real-time discursive flow). Data representing or reflecting on the actuality, artefacts, and/or participant accounts of practices, provide grounds for establishing interelateablity between practices. For site ontological interests, this forms an invaluable part of bridging the complex 'living' reality of the practice to the conclusions drawn by the researcher. A range of methods and techniques for gathering empirical data in and about the particular field of study are exemplified. The implications of the site ontological basis for researching practices, and in particular designing practice-based studies, are discussed. Specifically, we address how a main principle of a site ontological approach to research design is to ensure a focus on the situatedness, and so *happeningness*, of practices.

In the first two chapters of this book, we have outlined the related theories of practice architectures and ecologies of practices. In these previous chapters, we have briefly considered the importance of the locally situatedness, and so *site ontological* nature, of these practice theories. Together the theories treat practices as socially constituted (among people), dialogically formed (through language and communication), locally situated (as occurring in particular places), as ecologically interrelated (with other practices), and as accomplished in real-time happenings (in a real-time discursive flow). According to the theory of practice architectures, understanding the nature of practices demands attention to the realities of the kind of nuanced site-contingent activity accomplished by practitioners of practices. This view is distinct from an epistemological perspective that especially theorises knowledge and its acquisition, and often concerns more quantitative measures in its attention to methods, validity, and scope. This is not to say that one cannot fruitfully have an epistemological view of education and/or practice (a more dominant view in fields such as education and health), but following Carr and Kemmis (1986) and Schatzki (2002), among other practice theorists (or conceptualised in theories such as ethnomethodology or phenomenology), a site ontological perspective offered us a more fulsome scope for studying the day-to-day lived realities of the practices we were interested in.

In simple terms, for us, like other practice theorists, a site ontological perspective allows us to consider ways that the practices we are studying are inherently entangled in sites and the site-based conditions that enable and constrain what is actually happening. This means we, like other researchers, are oriented towards asking research questions that illuminate the cultural–discursive, material–economic and social–political arrangements that influence the conduct of practice as experienced in actual sites of study. In this chapter, we focus explicitly on how researching practices, through a practice architectures lens, requires research questions, study design, and data collection methods which attend to, and recognise, the situatedness of practices.

3.1 Site Ontologies and Social Practices

After Schatzki (2002) and Kemmis et al. (2014a), considering the existential (that which actually exists in time and physical space) and site ontological (where practices actually happen) dimensions of practice means grappling with understanding the specificities of practice sites. In their seminal text, Kemmis et al. (2014b) explained the importance of considering these dimensions, since

> the *site* – a classroom in a school in its community, for example—is always *the existential and ontological given* in education. It is the place where things happen—where people meet and engage with one another in practice amid the practice architectures that make those practices possible. The site of a practice is the phenomenological reality that always and necessarily escapes standardisation in curricula, standards, assessments and policies. (pp. 214–215)

For the theory of practice architectures, the site ontological view is a stance that draws attention to the robust complexities of particularity in terms of the lived realities and site-based conditions that influence the social orders and arrangements existing and entangled in actual sites or places where social practices happen. Such a view specifies the central importance of how in sites, 'the contingent, shifting, and fragile relations among social phenomena that weave them into everchanging constellations' (Schatzki, 2002, p. 2), and *hang together* in practices always situated in time and space. On this Schatzki (2002, p. 14) explains that 'human coexistence is a hanging-together of human lives that forms a context in which each proceeds individually in the practice', clarifying that 'a phenomenon is social, accordingly, when it pertains to human coexistence' (p. 169). Drawing on the German word *Zusammenhang* to describe the 'state of held togetherness' (2002, p. 14), Schatzki asserts that practices are the medium in which human lives interrelate or hang together. In this sense, practices always happen somewhere, held together (as *Zusammenhang*) in a nexus of interrelated practices as interlocutors, as social beings, come to participate in projects (like a science lessons, doctor-patient consultations about X-rays results, or an accountant–client meeting about a business plan).

Next, in this section we will address three key questions:

- What is site ontology?
- Why is site ontology vital to practice theory?
- How do we reconcile a 'theory' with a site ontological perspective?

After addressing these three questions, we will move onto specifically discussing empirical research design and practice from a site ontological perspective.

3.2 What is Site Ontology?

Fundamentally, a site ontological approach means focusing on what actually happens in particular sites; that is, what unfolds in real time and space. A site ontology can be understood as distinct from an ontology which refers to a way of being, sometimes relates to one's spirit, beliefs or cultural ways of being. The concept of site ontology is a general, yet more, formal representation of knowledge about a particular site or location. It can be used to describe the features and characteristics of a site, such as its geography, history, and cultural significance. Site ontologies are often used in archaeology and other fields that deal with the study of specific locations. According to the theory of practice architectures, a site ontological perspective is important because, in education for example, the site is where the actual education that learners and teachers experience. While, for example, teacher knowledge and beliefs are important, their significance is only because they may shape teaching practice, which only ever unfolds in real time–space in actual sites. So, in this sense, a site ontological approach centres on the actual *happeningness* of practices (in this example teaching); not what people think should happen; not ideas or theories about how learning and teaching occur; and, not the intentions of curricula. Together, these form part of the practice architectures that shape educational practices, but they are *not* the actual practices that are experienced. So, a site ontological approach is a focus on education practices (or whatever the field of interest) *as* it happens.

The concept of *the site* is crucial; and thus needs some further explication. First, 'the site' is not the same thing as 'the context',[1] albeit that some people may use these terms interchangeably. The site is an ontological term that refers to the substantive

---

[1] Context refers in more general terms, to the background, environment, setting, framework, or typical surroundings of events or occurrences; for instance, classrooms, in a generic sense, are a typically understood as contexts where teaching and learning happen, and are recognisably such that people understand the classroom as context.

and qualitative beingness of a specific place; that is, an actual place and time where practices occur. For example, this could be a specific physical classroom or particular meeting room in a particular accountancy firm, but equally it could be a virtual learning space conducted via Zoom, or an online Teams meeting. Furthermore, in any particular site there can be a range of practices occurring simultaneously, and as outlined in the previous chapter, to a greater or lesser degree these will be ecologically arranged. It is the particular site where specific practitioners meet one another as interlocutors in semantic space, in physical time–space, and in social space. For example, the practice of participating in an end of financial meeting among an accountancy firm's executive will unfold in real time as participants might attend in person in an actual boardroom, or attend via online media; where they might be physically sitting in their workplace offices at their computer, and where relatedly, the sociality of that multidimensional site is determined by furnishings or a particular social media platform; and where in the semantic space of their shared connection to accountancy, they use specific discourses and language (e.g., fiscal responsibility, ledgers, cost accounting, cash flow, auditing, taxation laws).

3.2.1 Three Senses of Site

Schatzki (2002) was particularly influential for the concepts framing the theory of practice architectures. His distinction, differentiating three interconnected nested genres, or 'senses of the site' (2002, p. 63), is important to counter and delimit more narrow 'spatial connotations of 'where'' (2002, p. 63), while recognising that conditions outside the particular place also influence the unfolding of practices in real time–space. To this end,

- the *first sense of site* focuses on the specific, immediate, spatial location where practices occur. For example, the actual teaching and learning that happens in the moment-by-moment as a lesson unfolds in a particular physical space like a classroom;
- the *second sense of site* concerns the wider context or local realm in which practices exist. For example, a classroom is in a particular school, which in turn is placed in a specific community, where teachers make available the curriculum to students; and,
- the *third sense of site* relates to the broader space, field, or domain which the practice is intrinsically located. For example, teaching and learning occurs within the prevailing educational policies and generic frameworks, and within the jurisdiction of a governing authority (adapted from Schatzki, 2002, pp. 63–64).

The theory of practice architectures pays close attention to the relationship and distinctions between the micro, meso, and macro *'senses of the site'* since each is a practice architecture for the other. This is captured in the nested nature of practices and practice architectures, as outlined in the previous chapter describing ecologies of practices. Orienting to the three senses of the site clearly shows the complexly interconnected arrangement of practices, and assists in developing a more nuanced and particular understanding of the term 'the site', and perhaps distinguishes it from more general terms such as context, place, or landscape. These insights raise the importance and necessity for understanding practices in terms of their precise site ontological character, because outside of a site-specific comprehension, they have limited meaning or value apart from in the most general sense.

These ideas have a range of implications for research, but returning to the notion of 'best practice' (discussed in Chap. 1) a site-specific understanding of practices renders the term nothing but an elusive myth. As Grootenboer (2018) argued, this pervasive notion of 'best practice' (in education for example) is, at best, a generalised aspiration, and at worst, a dangerous hegemonic discourse that restricts effective and site-responsive practices. A site ontological practice approach means that, beyond the most general of abstractions, there is no formulaic, generic or uniform 'best practice', because each local site has its own circumstances and conditions that form the practice architectures that shapes what is possible in any particular place, and also among the wider place of practice, and amidst the wider social, political, and cultural conditions of the broader field.

3.2.2 Why is Site Ontology Vital to Practice Theory[2]?

We acknowledge that not all 'practice theories' are based on a site ontological approach—for example, the seminal work of Gherardi (2008) is more epistemological in nature. However, the theory of practice architectures is clearly and intentionally site ontological, where a main focus is on the *happeningness* of practice. The idea of happeningness is essential because it keeps central the dynamism of life, as it is lived, in practices. This is not to eschew knowledge and thinking, or beliefs and values, or identity, emotions and feelings, but rather orients the researcher to *see* these as expressed, or made relevant, in the activity of practices in time and space (Grootenboer & Edwards-Groves, 2019). Thus, the essence of considering the situatedness of practices demands consideration be equally given to practices as they happen; that is, unfolding in real time and actual spaces as people are relating and interacting. This central emphasis shifts the notions of examining practices towards coming to see and understand knowledge, identity, beliefs, and emotions *as* they are revealed in the sayings, doings, and relatings comprising practice.

As we have noted previously, this provides a refreshing way to view social phenomenon, particularly since many researchers focus on epistemological features like knowledge, or intrapersonal features like identity, beliefs, and emotions, or characterising features like attributes, traits, qualities, temperaments, and dispositions. Shifting attention to the happeningness of practices takes some readjustment of focus. Nevertheless, in our view it is crucial, not for the least reason that we can actually only

---

[2] In our writing, we often describe happeningness as in-the-moment, or then-and there unfolding of practices.

access what someone might think, know, belief or feel through their practices—there is no way of looking into heads or hearts to have a firsthand gaze at these things.

The concept of happeningness of practices means that they can only be understood in particular sites at particular times. Thus, the practice architectures that enable and constrain any particular practice are site-specific, and although at times they might be broad and general (e.g., a government policy) they can only be realised and experienced at a particular site at a particular time since the conditions and arrangements (there and then) are unique to each practice site. Hence, a site ontological positioning necessitates researching and understanding practices as locally situated (i.e., site specific in time and space). For example, while we can talk about broad practices like leadership, and even perhaps recognise some common characteristics that might define leadership practices, these are often generically portrayed in policy documentation or in 'practice traditions' of leading—since the actual practices of leading can only be realised and unfold then-and-there on occasions of leading. Further to this, taking a site ontological view renders more precision to what leading practices might be happening, since even when the same person might be exercising leading in two different locations, their actual leading practices would be considered as different and uniquely connect to the site of practice because each site has its own practice architectures—the focus is the leading practices, not the leader traits per se.

What is clear here is that practices, and the site-based practice architectures that enable and constrain them, are mutually constitutive, and as such, they evolve symbiotically as they unfold in time and space. Thus, a site ontological approach also sees practices as temporal and dynamic—practices and the associated practice architectures are changing together, as are the other ecologically arranged practices in the site, chronologically. Again, this is important because this is how real life is experienced, and so while we try to label and describe things as static or fixed, we can actually only capture a snapshot representation of them at a particular time and place. Of course, this is valuable and useful, particularly as we try to understand and develop practices, but it is an unavoidable limitation of researching practices from a site ontological standpoint. Nevertheless, it does perhaps offer greater value that trying to somehow ascertain what this might mean for the qualities and characteristics of practitioners as hermeneutically determined by inference from practices or through dialogue, because it is closer to existential and phenomenological nature of life.

3.2.3 How Do We Reconcile a 'Theory' with a Site Ontological Perspective?

Before moving onto looking at researching from a site ontological perspective, it is worth briefly addressing the apparent contradiction of a theory—which by nature is epistemological, of practice, which we have argued is site ontological. The theory of practice architectures, and the associated theory of ecologies of practices, are epistemological models or conceptions of practice—but they are not themselves *practices.* The reading of theory can be a practice; the writing of theory can be a practice; but the theory itself is not a practice, and hence it is epistemological in nature, and not site ontological.

3.3 Researching Practices in Sites

In this next section we will look at what it means to research practices in sites, because, given the site ontological nature of practices, there is no other way to really do it! Researching and understanding practices needs to focus on their *happening*, and they happen in mutually constitutive ways with the practice architectures in the site. Thus, the crux of the research is to comprehend *the site*. Of course, this is complex and demands an intense and broad and interrelated view of the practices of interest.

As a prefatory caution, sometimes we have read studies that have employed the theory of practice architectures, where it seems a fundamental concern is on identifying the 'sayings, doings, and relatings' of the practice(s), and the 'cultural–discursive, material–economic, and social–political' arrangements. While it is usually relevant to do these things (at least as a preliminary step), in and of itself it is not really a study of practices and practice architectures—just their constituent 'bits'. To simply point these things out, alone, is of limited interest or value to understanding the complexity of sites. Moreover, isolating the 'sayings, doings, and relatings' is only meaningful when they are considered as integral and interrelated components of a practice, realised in the pursuit of a project—on this, therefore, the unit of analysis is the practice as it pertains the interrelationship between the three senses of a site. Similarly, for the practice architectures—while the dimensions of the arrangements can be identified, they only make sense as a whole. Furthermore, while it is also possible to investigate and discuss practices and practice architectures independently, their site ontological nature mean that it really only makes sense to consider them together and in a complex interrelated manner. At this point, it is clear to say that researching practice is neither simple, easy, or straight forward!

The other key feature that is important to note here is about capturing the *happeningness* of practices in research. A site ontological perspective requires a phenomenological and existential approach to research where the focus is on what occurs, rather than practitioners' beliefs or theories about the phenomenon—in essence, data has to be about *what is*, rather than what could or should be, or ideas about what might be. Of course, this has significant implications for research design and data collection, discussed next.

3.4 Designing Practice-Based Research

This section presents specific ideas and practical insights for designing and conducting research into practices, particularly using the theory of practice architectures. Importantly, as we consider how research into practices might be undertaken, we are guided by the principles outlined in the beginning of this chapter, and the preceding two chapters.

3.4.1 Situating Practice—Implications for Data Gathering

A central concern for those researching practices relates to the extent to which the collected data arises from and informs an inherent interest in the site. Therefore, aligned with Schatzki's three senses of site (introduced above), the researcher must begin with implementing practice-oriented methods that assign understanding about ways practices are always situated (i) in moment-by-moment discursive and interactional activity, (ii) in places amidst local needs and circumstances (e.g., accounting for geography, demography), and (iii) within broader domains, fields, traditions, or disciplines (e.g., education, health, or accountancy). A site ontological leaning, thus, insists that the theory of practice architectures is put to work in qualitative research by which researchers gather information about the tripartite sense of sites in ways that allows empirical material (gathered of observations and accounts of practices) to be turned into analysable data (Freebody, 2003).

Assigning prominence to the site and the intrinsically situatedness of practices requires the researcher to use data-gathering methods that draw attention to, and produce more precise information about:

1. the three senses of site (in the moment like a lesson, a doctor–patient consultation, or an annual general meeting; in the place or context like a school in rural community, a doctor's surgery in a large regional town outer-city suburb, or in a large accountancy firm in an inner-city business district; and in the domain or field like in education, health, or business);
2. ways specific sayings, doings, and relatings 'in motion' in specific projects of a practice (like a mathematics lesson, a medical consultation, or a business meeting) are enabled and constrained by practice architectures; and,
3. the reciprocal relationship between practice architectures and practices that happen there and then, at that place, in this field.

Establishing complexity comprising the conduct of social life, brought off by practices experienced as sayings, doings, and relatings always-in-motion in their happening, 'can be reconfigured such that it is able to be rendered into the stuff of research—such that practices as 'living entities' become the 'findings" (adapted from Freebody, 2003, p. 28). Thus, data gathering and the analysis of it resides primarily in examining observations of actual practice as it unfolds in real-time, the artefacts which inform and arise from the practice, and participant's accounts of practice.

Together, data representing or reflecting on the actuality, artefacts, and/or participant accounts of practices provide grounds for establishing interelateablity which arises from a robust body of evidence that admits convergence, contestation, and corroboration. For site ontological interests, this forms an invaluable part of bridging the complex 'living' reality of the practice to the conclusions drawn by the researcher. These three distinct foci are accompanied by a range of methods and techniques for gathering empirical data in and about the particular field of study; examples of each are outlined in the next subsections.

3.4.2 Actuality of Practice

Observational data are precisely of value because they focus on naturally occurring activities. Since, in reality, practices are not static and unfold in real-time activity in physical space, capturing the in-situ dynamism of the *happeningness* of practices is crucial (Schatzki, 2010). Thus, the appropriate empirical centre of inquiry for studies focused on understanding practices is the study of actual practices 'as they happen', not, by themselves, substitutes such as what researchers code in their observations, or what practitioners bring to bear in describing or evaluating the practice at the centre of the study, or how a particular theory or policy pre-empts the nature and efficacy of the practice (Edwards-Groves et al., 2022). Transcripts of recorded observations (for example) are an important technology for studying practices since they reveal 'the collaborative ways in which members manage their conduct and their circumstances to achieve the orderly features of their activities' (Boden & Zimmerman, 1991, p. 7). So, in understanding practices, there is a need for determination in order to identify the phenomenon in situ, and to understand that its location is separated from the practice only to render the conclusions invalid (Freebody, 2003).

Collecting data records of practices as they are happening temporally in real time is an essential feature of practice-based research.

Examples of data include:

- field notes of participant and non-participant observations (lessons, professional development meetings, the consultation, and the training session),
- audio- and/or video-recordings of observations where recordings can be transcribed for analytic purposes,
- researcher, professional, and/or participant generated transcripts of audio- and/or video-recordings of observations, researcher and/or participant photographs of activity, and shadowing.

In researching practice, to support digital recordings (that later are often turned into transcripts for analysis), it is important to take detailed written (minuted) field notes, and include (if possible, and relevant to the research question or study design) photographs, drawing spatial maps of the physical space (furniture, tables, and participants), and/or topographical drawings of the space when accompanied with recordings. Noting the discourses, physical set ups, materiality, embodiment (e.g., proximity, gaze, gesture), and different interactional configurations across the courses of action can form part of the data gathering, allowing the researcher to pay attention to there-and-then practices. Throughout the period of observation, it is worth noting concrete instances (including timings) of how people are using the physical space and use of material resources in their activity. These supplement the collection of other relevant data and may provide useful insights of practice architectures that can later be explored. Sometimes using precoded observation schedules as a guide, provides additional data that allow more comprehensive descriptions to be made rather than rely on recall or impressions about what is happening.

3.4.3 Artefacts of Practice

Collecting artefacts in the form of public records, personal documents or texts, or other relevant physical objects and resources found within the study setting that inform, influence, and arise from a practice and the analysis of these is an important feature of social practice research. As a qualitative method its own right, an analysis of artefacts can contribute to understanding and explaining practices as these are indeed elements of the practice architectures which prefigure what happens and how practitioners themselves understand the nature of their work. Decoding and analysing texts, artefacts, objects, or products of practice, and other documents involves coding content into themes, categories or subjects (Bowen, 2009). (See in the next chapter, a description of using for example a table of invention as a mapping tool or rubric that can help to organise data in ways that distil and delineate the factors concerning sayings, doings, and relatings and the cultural–discursive, material–economic, and social–political arrangements that influence practices).

Examining three primary types of texts, documents, or objects that inform or arise from the actual practice and practice architectures under study (O'Leary, 2014) is important. Note, we exclude the artefacts of research such as recording or transcripts of interview or observation data.

Examples of data include:

- *Public records*: official school and system policy documents, curriculum and syllabi, frameworks and guidelines, ongoing records of an organisation's activities (minutes of meetings), student transcripts, mission statements, annual reports, policy manuals, strategic plans, transcripts, statements of purpose, yearly reports, strategy manuals, historical texts and records, handbooks, government policy, media reports, social media, and websites.
- *Personal documents or texts*: student and teacher work samples, teacher annotated work samples, student assessment records, photographs of student generated work products (sculptures, paintings, drawings, written texts, digital texts, models, story

maps, dioramas, etc.), meeting notes, calendars, e-mails, scrapbooks, workbooks, blogs, Facebook posts, other social media, duty logs, incident reports, reflections/journals/diaries, online journals, date-books, messages, program logs, occurrence reports, and/or daily notations and associated papers (or photographs of these).
- *Physical layouts, objects, resources, and other evidence found within the study site*: spatial maps, birds-eye view plans or drawings, flyers, posters, professional publications, wall plans, agendas, and/or handbooks, handouts, and training materials (or photographs of these).

These sources of data can be particularly useful in understanding the practice architectures that enable and constrain practice possibilities in any given site.

3.4.4 Accounts of Practice

Eliciting participant accounts of practices is a commonly used method of inquiry in practice-based qualitative research that can be documented through the retellings and representations of actions or experiences and the expression of opinions, perspectives, or beliefs. They are important of establishing how participants construe the significance and nature of the practices in which they are part, and provide a forum for communicating personal histories, predispositions, reactions, prejudices, bias, and emotions that can arise in the unfolding of a practice, or indeed form practice architectures for 'practicing in the present'. Participant accounts further assist the researcher to come to more fulsome understandings about a participant's sense of agency, solidarity, and power in the circumstances in which they find themselves. However, that said, it is crucial that the data gathered or created through these methods has a clear focus on practice and what happened historically, not participants theories or beliefs about the practice generally.

Examples of data include:

- first-person accounts of an individual's descriptions and exemplification of practices, actions, opinions, perspectives, experiences, and/or beliefs
- survey—semi-structured or structured questionnaires
- audio- and/or video-recorded, and then transcribed, interviews and focus groups (conducted as part of a three-part taxonomy, or question–answer sequence, Freebody (2003).
- other approaches include informal conversations (recorded in anecdotal field notes or include audio- and/or video-recordings), photo-stimulated recall interviews, photo-voice, participant creative representations of their practices, actions, opinions, perspectives, experiences, and/or beliefs recorded in concept maps, mind maps, diagrams, photographs, poetry, or artworks.

Interviews and focus groups are generally conducted along a continuum of formality in the form of structured, semi-structured or open-ended interviews with a range of stakeholders such as teachers, students, principals, consumers, patients, clients, managers, parents, or community members.

3.4.5 Some Words of Caution

However, a study of practice must account for the site ontological nature of happeningness, where the focus is on the work that practices are taken to do in 'real time' or as Schatzki (2010) says 'in activity space–time'. So, 'on any given occasion in a practice, what is said and how participants relate to one another in the doing of an activity is available then and there to the participants (and thereby to the researcher), while the intentions, thoughts and histories of speakers (and hearers) are not' (Edwards-Groves et al., 2022, p. 97). This means that using proxy methods alone (e.g., interviews or policy analysis) outside of the situation and the happeningness of practice, 'the specific details of naturally situated interactional conduct are irretrievably lost and are replaced by idealisations about how interaction [and so practice] works' (Heritage, 1984, p. 236). Of course, there is the inevitability of loss, even through the perceptive nature of first-hand methods, but nevertheless, time in the actual site is very valuable. Thus, even with its ethical challenges, recording and documenting the occasioned interactional discursive work in practice is important identifying the practice architectures that contribute to developing contextually bound information about what, when, and how that particular practice is being produced, reproduced, or transformed in particular sites.

Although there is an inherent merit in eliciting accurate 'true' and 'felt' accounts of practice through the conduct of interviews or focus groups, cautionary notes concerning the deceptive complexity of 'the interview' must be recognised (Edwards-Groves & Freebody, 2022; Freebody, 2003, 2021). First, while it is laudable to attempt to equalise the researcher-participant relationship, it must be recognised that there is always an asymmetry in the interactional rights between them (Hughes, 1982, p. 369). Second interviews can be understood in two ways: (i) interviews as building participant accounts and (ii) interviews as an interactive event. The interview itself is an interactive interpersonal exchange—a practice, thus is subject to the practice architectures of the interview as a site of practice; for example, accounts can be influenced depending of the degrees of latitude afforded by the interviewer, how the participant takes up or follows the line of thought, the questioning style, the recency of the participant's actual involvement in the practice under study, the conditions under which the accounts are expressed, or the fidelity of focus (by the interviewer and interviewee). Therefore, an overreliance on the accounts of practice (for example), without accompanying/supplementary observations of practitioners practising or gathering the relevant materials or policy documents which shape their practices, limits a researcher's capacity to document the actual realities of practices as unfolding in real time or those particular practice architectures instituted by particular policy demands which simultaneously prefigure their in-the-moment practising. Therefore, in research practices themselves, there is a need to alleviate this limitation in the interview by prioritising a practice focus with a persistent determination to elicit concrete examples of practices, and establishing the *enablements and* constraints experienced by participants, since this an inherent interest for those using the theory. Finally, the disadvantages of gathering and using an analysis of artefacts alone are countered when triangulated with in-situ observations and accounts (Bowen, 2009).

To counter limitations drawn out here, many researchers using the theory of practice architectures generally rely on a combination of these methodologies to make reliable textual representations and re-productions of sites, practices and participant activity in those sites and practices. When used together, rather than diffuse the robustness of participant accounts, transcripts of the activity of practice that accompany such accounts provide a stronger near-to-practice empirical basis for making claims about the multidimensionality and complexity of practices.

Although each of these methodological constellations have merit, intent, and emphasis in their own right, the use of at least two different data sources provides a scheme for triangulation necessary for instilling confidence and credibility in their interpretation and conclusions (Mertens & Hesse-Biber, 2012; Wiersma, 1995). To promote internal reliability, studies of practices importantly present disconfirming and anomalous evidence along with commonalities and convergences to avoid issues associated with seamless glossed 'one-story one-voice' accounts of practices (Freebody, 2003). For example, in critical ethnographic research (see Kemmis et al., 2014c), the use of multiple data sources forms the basis for in-depth descriptive studies of practices and their ecological interdependencies since data are strengthened and triangulated across the sources giving insight into the site-based conditions which enable *and* constrain practices across multiple occasions of practising.

3.4.6 Research Design

In this section we are not going to describe all the usual important considerations that need to be attended to in designing a research study (there are already many good books that do that!). Rather, we specifically consider how a site ontological practice-based study influences study design and the kinds of research questions that might be asked. In short, the main principle is to ensure a focus on the situatedness, and so *happeningness*, of practices.

3.4.7 Research Questions

Given that the theoretical framework for the study has already been determined (i.e., the theory of practice architectures and the theory of ecologies of practices), then the next part of the research design is to consider the research questions. Not surprisingly, given all that has gone before, these questions need to focus on practices—not practitioners per se, but the practices and associated practice architectures themselves. Thus, questions will be about teaching practices rather than teachers; nursing practices rather than nurses; and, accounting practices rather than accountants, albeit that these practices are enacted by people. This is not necessarily difficult or profound, but it does require an attunement to a site ontological conception of practice.

To illustrate, recently we undertook a study into educational middle leading practices in school sites, with the intention of uncovering and understanding this largely unresearched area. For this study our over-arching research question was: *what are educational middle leading practices?* This question is about practice which centred on what middle leaders actually did—something we had very little empirical evidence about. This was then underpinned by two related subquestions:

1. What middle leading practices facilitate strategic curriculum delivery and drive effective pedagogical practices in site-based teaching teams?
2. How do the leading practices of middle leaders' impact teaching *and* student learning practices?

These two research questions were designed to further investigate how educational middle leading practices created practice architectures for teacher professional development practices and student learning practices, and specifically how all these practices are ecologically arranged in school sites. In this example you can see that the research questions do not focus on the personal qualities or knowledge of the middle leaders, or the teachers, or the learning outcomes per se of the students. These research questions were then investigated using the methods that have been outlined in the previous section, including video- and audio-recorded observations, shadowing, dialogue conferences, interviews and focus groups post observations, collection of artefacts, online interviews about what middle leaders do, and a questionnaire about the middle leaders' practices.

3.4.8 Research Methodologies

The theory of practice architectures is not a research methodology, but it does lend itself to some research methodologies more than others. Often, when trying to apprehend how practices unfold in a particular site, it requires a longitudinal approach, particularly so the ecological arrangements between practices can be understood. Below we list a few methodologies that have commonly been used in researching practices.

- *Case study.* Case studies, or collective case studies, have been widely used by researchers who have employed the theory of practice architectures. This is because this approach is particularly amenable to site-based research, where the practices of interest are unfolding in a specific site at a specific time. Case studies

are also attentive to particular conditions and arrangements of the 'case' because the research is centred on a particular site.
- *Action research.* The essence of action research is to critically analyse practices in a particular site, and then to change them through an iterative cyclic process. As such, *action* research could probably more accurately be called *practice* research (Kemmis et al., 2014b), because the focus is actually about changing human practices. For a detailed and practical discussion of undertaking practice-based research through action research read the seminal text by Kemmis et al. (2014b). An example of research using critical participatory action research and practice theory is the Edwards-Groves and Rönnerman study studying the longer-term impacts of action research on learning to lead (see Edwards-Groves & Rönnerman, 2013, 2021; Rönnerman & Edwards-Groves, 2012).
- *Design-based research.* This is a specific type of action research which is more focused and directed, and it is compatible with a practice approach when the *design* is a practice or related set of practices.
- *Critical ethnography.* The theory of practice architectures can be use in ethnographic studies in order to describe the practices that are unfolding in a particular place and over time, where deep insights about sites can be revealed through such studies. Since the theory focuses on specific in-situ practices and the conditions and arrangements that enable and constrain them (i.e., the practice architectures), then it can facilitate the uncovering of interdependent practices and unjust social inequities. For example, the four-year 'Leading and Learning' project published in *Changing practices, changing education* (Kemmis et al., 2014c) has been described as a critical ethnography for its focused and deep empirically enriched attention to interelateablity between practices and practice architectures.

3.5 Concluding Comments

In this chapter, we have outlined how a research study into practices might be undertaken. In the first two chapters, the theoretical and philosophical grounding of the theory of practice architectures, and the associated theory of ecologies of practices, were outlined, and so here we could look at what this means for research. From our experience, often the hardest aspect to grasp, particularly in considering research, is the site ontological nature of practices, and the required mindset shift from an epistemological approach to research. As we have outlined, a site ontological perspective orients the researcher to the happeningness of practices in particular sites at particular times, and so the associated research design and data collection methods need to also be focused on this crucial feature. The data collection/generation methods outlined in this chapter were illustrated and discussed to illustrate in pragmatic ways how this might be done, and this now leads into the next chapter where we discuss data analysis vis-à-vis the theory of practice architectures.

References

Boden, D., & Zimmerman, D. (1991). *Talk and social structure: Studies in ethnomethodology and conversation analysis*. University of California Press

Bowen, G. A. (2009). Document analysis as a qualitative research method. *Qualitative Research Journal, 9*, 27–40.

Carr, W., & Kemmis, S. (1986). *Becoming critical: Knowledge and action research*. Falmer Press.

Edwards-Groves, C., & Freebody, P. (2022). Literacy's changing morphologies: Trajectories, classroom exchanges and the evolution of literacy demands over the school years. *Australian Journal of Language and Literacy, 44*(2), 76–89.

Edwards-Groves, C., Garoni, S., & Freebody, P. (2022). Transitions in literacy and classroom interaction across the school years. In P.T. Jones, E. Matruglio & C. Edwards-Groves (Eds.) *Transition and continuity in school literacy development*. Bloomsbury.

Edwards-Groves, C., & Rönnerman, K. (2013). Generating leading practices through professional learning. *Professional Development in Education, 39*(1), 122–140.

Edwards-Groves, C., & Rönnerman, K. (2021). *Generative leadership: Rescripting the promise of action research*. Springer.

Edwards-Groves, C., Wilkinson, J., & Mahon, K. (2020). Leading as shared transformational practice. In Mahon, K., Edwards-Groves, C., Francisco, S., Kaukko, M., Kemmis, S., & Petrie, K. (Eds), *Pedagogy, Education, and Praxis in Critical Times*, (pp. 117–141). Springer.

Freebody, P. (2003). *Qualitative research in education: Interaction and practice*. Sage.

Freebody, P. (2021). Portraits of 'learning on the move': Teachers' accounts of literacy's trajectories. *Australian Journal of Language and Literacy, 44*(2), 26–36.

Gherardi, S. (2008). Situated knowledge and situated action: What do practice-based studies promise? In D. Barry & H. Hansen (Eds.), *The SAGE handbook of new approaches in organization and management* (pp. 516–525). Sage Publications.

Grootenboer, P. (2018). *The practices of school middle leadership: Leading professional learning*. Springer.

Grootenboer, P., & Edwards-Groves, C. (2019). Learning mathematics as being stirred into mathematical practices: an alternative perspective on identity formation. In Special issue "Identity in mathematical education", *ZDM Mathematics Education, 5*, 1–12

Hughes, D. (1982). Control in the medical consultation. *Sociology, 16*(3), 359–376.

Kemmis, S., Heikkinen, H. L. T., Fransson, G., Aspfors, J., & Edwards-Groves, C. (2014a). Mentoring of new teachers as a contested practice: Supervision, support and collaborative self-development. *Teaching and Teacher Education, 43*, 154–164.

Kemmis, S., McTaggart, R., & Nixon, R. (2014b). *The action research planner: Doing critical participatory action research*. Springer.

Kemmis, S., Wilkinson, J., Edwards-Groves, C., Hardy, I., Grootenboer, P., & Bristol, L. (2014c). *Changing practices*. Springer.

Mertens, D., & Hesse-Biber, S. (2012). Triangulation and mixed methods research: Provocative positions. *Journal of Mixed Methods Research, 6*(2), 75–79.

O'Leary, Z. (2014). *The essential guide to doing your research project* (2nd ed.). SAGE Publications.

Rönnerman, K., & Edwards-Groves, C. (2012). Genererat ledarskap [Generative Leadership]. In K. Rönnerman (Ed.), *Aktionsforskning i praktiken – förskola och skola på vetenskaplig grund*. [*Action Research in Practice*] (pp. 171–190). Studentlitteratur.

Schatzki, T. R. (2002). *The site of the social: A philosophical account of the constitution of social life and change*. Pennsylvania State University Press.

Schatzki, T. R. (2010). *The timespace of human activity: On performance, society, and history as indeterminate teleological events*. Lexington.

Wiersma, W. (1995). *Research methods in education: An introduction*. Allyn & Bacon.

Chapter 4
Studying Practices: Interpreting and Analysing Data

Abstract This chapter addresses the study of practice within a *practice paradigm* that suggests the legitimacy of the evidence and, according to the theory of practice architectures, the interpretation of it must centre on practices and their practice architectures. This idea is necessary since the basic unit of analysis is practices. Specifically, the chapter provides examples of some analytic approaches that support researchers interpret and analyse data, including creating practice webs as an organisational frame to show the interrelationships between practices and practitioners, transcript analysis, interaction analysis, thematic analysis, and table of invention (which can be used as a framing or mapping tool). We stress the importance that when analysing practices, the three practice dimensions (sayings, doings, and relatings) and the practice architectures (cultural–discursive, material–economic, and social–political) are drawn apart for analytic purposes, but noting that in reality, they are always interwoven, connected-at-all-points.

The domains of inquiry in the field of practice are comparably varied and spread broadly across everyday domestic and professional sites, yet understanding the complex local factors at work remains a general point of interest. Therefore, the study of practice needs to locate itself both in the broad theoretical and specific practical domains in which it aims to play a part. This chapter addresses the study of practice within a *practice paradigm* that suggests the legitimacy of the evidence and, according to the theory of practice architectures, the interpretation of it must centre on practices and their practice architectures since the basic unit of analysis is practices. Thus, studying practices involves deconstructing, reconstructing, and historicising practices as they are configured, interpreted, and experienced by those involved—the practitioners of practices (Edwards-Groves & Rönnerman, 2021; Hardy & Edwards-Groves, 2016; Kemmis et al., 2014). The theory of practice architectures maintains that studying practices encompasses two interpretive tracks:

(i) the close analysis of intricately interconnected sayings, doings, and relatings which configure a practice then-and there, and
(ii) locating the practice (being studied) within broader interrelated cultural–discursive, material–economic, and social–political arrangements that influence *how*,

why, and *to what extent* practices of certain kinds are produced, reproduced, and transformed in (real) time and over (historical) time.

Thus, 'getting at' the details of practices necessarily means attending to, or at least, recognising the entirety of the practicescape. In this chapter, the focus is on interpreting and analysing data with the theory of practice architectures guiding this critical empirically driven part of the research process. It responds to questions about how the researcher can foreground the particularity of a practice, yet, at the same time, not let attention to the practice architectures escape in their interpretive and analytic work.

4.1 Interpreting Practices as Practical Activity in the World

For researchers drawing on the theory of practice architectures, a central focus of the interpretive work requires noticing, delineating, specifying, and problematising practice architectures in practices. This includes tracing the historical, ecological, and site ontological conditions that have bearing on—or enable and constrain—the *there-and-then* conduct of practices, *and reciprocally* identifying the relationship between specific dimensions of practices (its sayings, doings, and relatings) and the practice architectures that influence what is happening. However, as Freebody (2003, p. 28) reminds us:

> It is important to appreciate that the research process entails a series of practical activities in the world: observations, analysis and reporting. Because of that, all human research entails certain moments at which the phenomena, as they are experienced and observed by the researcher, are distilled, that is reduced and distorted. The question is always: Is there in these reductive and distorting processes enough to unmoor the finding from the original question and is this enough to make the conclusion insecure? Whatever the consequences of this process of distillation, it necessarily involves the researcher deciding which artefacts are most and least important: some features of the phenomenon are given more importance that others; some are either omitted or simply not seen; some phenomena become 'findings', and not others.

With these questions and consequences in mind, a site ontological approach to the study of practice directs the researcher towards seeking out and understanding its resolute 'localness'. Importantly, this has the added benefit of enhancing the internal validity of the research. But, as Freebody also cautioned, 'in doing this we make the addition of interpretations from this to other apparently, supposedly, or potentially comparable events more tenuous' (p. 29). It is critical, therefore, that the basic unit of analysis is *practice* itself (and thus its composite features—sayings, doings and relatings *and* the practice architectures that influence it), not simply or solely on what a practitioner thinks, interprets, says, feels, and does, outside the actual occasion of practicing.

The theory of practice architectures, like practice theories in the main, attempt to steer away from misleading ideas that by simply eliciting practitioner accounts or observing, then describing, the activities of the practical world—one gets closer to 'reality'. 'This is naïve empiricism—not simply about capturing what people do' (Nicolini, 2012, p. 7). Here we arrive at a problematic point that constantly presents itself in practice-based research—that because practices always occur in complex, local settings, amid multifaceted interconnected cultural–discursive, material–economic, and social–political arrangements, establishing clear understandings of practices in precise or resolute terms is always challenging.

To counter this challenge, what matters, for us, is getting a close-enough interpretation of the practicescape by taking account of the actual locally encountered site-based exigencies and contingencies of any given practice in light of particular practice arrangements. This requires empirical observations of both the happeningness (how the sayings, doings and relatings that comprise practices unfold temporally in real time, in the actual physical space being studied) *and* explicitly uncovering of the distinctiveness of site ontological conditions (the practice architectures that include practice traditions and policy settings bearing down on the practice at a particular place in a particular occasion of practicing).

4.1.1 The Complexity of Interpreting Practices in Sites: Practice Inside Out

Taking account of the multidimensionality, messiness and often disorderliness of practice, requires a concerted attempt at fidelity to the conceptual features of the respective theory, so that relative—close-enough to reality—sensemaking is achieved. Thus, clarity around the analytic approach applied to the interpretation of data (a point taken up later in this chapter) is necessary for yielding a true-enough description of the practicescape. Although, a researcher's attention may shift their points of distillation along different focal or highly specialised points of interest (e.g., participant agency in practice, policy discourses influencing practice, materiality affecting practice, solidarity in community activist groups, or the hierarchies of power in particular organisations).

4.1.1.1 Considerations for Entering the Research Practice Zone

Bringing systematic analysis to the messiness of practice is a complex challenge for the researcher, this in simple terms cannot be completely avoided. However, some simple considerations can be taken to negotiate the complexity of interpreting practices in sites.

1. Data capture must cut underneath the surface of more obvious descriptions of a saying, a doing, a relating, for example, to sharpen the focus on eliciting the distinguishing peculiarities and distinctiveness about what is happening at any given time.

2. Begin with focusing on the observable—recording what can be seen and heard (field notes and recordings which can be transcribed as artefacts), mapping the observation setting itself—then practice architectures can emerge more comprehensively through interviews and policy tracing etc.
3. Try to avoid what is not observable at the time, like perceived intentions, motivations, participant attitudes or thoughts.
4. The researcher must remain sensitised to a practice stance by attending to, drawing apart and examining the practices and the interrelated practice architectures present, but also following the *red thread* to trace the history (genesis and evolution) of those practices and practice architectures (Edwards-Groves & Rönnerman, 2021; Edwards-Groves & Hardy, 2013).
5. In interviews, for example, the key line of questioning should remain faithful to illuminating practices (what is happening) and practice architectures (what is influencing those happenings), where human dispositions, emotions, and feelings emerge from the retellings of experiences of practices.
6. Try to avoid more basic descriptive analysis that produces reductionist accounts of practices by simply describing sayings, doings, and relatings (although this is entirely appropriate for a first wave of analysis, and critical for yielding a preliminary view of the practice); while these categories may be commonsensical, on the one hand; on the other, without a deeper dive into the empirical material there is a danger of simply glossing more comprehensive and nuanced understandings of the practicescape under investigation.

4.2 Analysis of Practices

This section addresses a perennial question asked of the use of the theory of practice architectures concerning the processes, methods, and rigour of analysis. As Freebody (2003, p. x) said 'For researchers, methods need to be generative of significant reflection, not just equipment for producing simplistic conclusions'. Thus, a range of data sources (as outlined in the previous chapter), methods, and analyses (summarised in Table 4.1) are used to allow the researcher to analyse different dimensions of practices and practice architectures, and to synthesise how practices are variously enmeshed with arrangements *in* sites, and *as* sites, yielding deeply rich *case studies of practices*. It is important to keep in mind that this chapter presents a necessarily condensed version of ways to approach interpreting and analysing empirical data, and dealing with findings (addressed in more detail in the next section).

It is important to note that the three practices dimensions (sayings, doings, and relatings) and the practice architectures (cultural–discursive, material–economic, and social–political) are drawn apart for analytic purposes, but in reality, they are always interwoven, and connected-at-all-points. Caution about interpretive selectivity or cherry-picking data to suit researcher bias or present a simple view of practices (e.g., collecting samples of sayings, or doings, or relatings and assigning them relevance

4.2 Analysis of Practices

Table 4.1 Data sources, methods, and analyses

Practices	Practice architectures	Accessed via (a) principal data gathering techniques and (b) analyses
Finding sayings in practice	*Cultural–discursive arrangements* (in *semantic space*)	(a) Participant and non-participant observation (what is said—the discourses and language used discursively in 'real time'); interviews and focus groups (participants' interpretations of sayings, participants use of the practice-related discourses and language in their accounts—explanations, descriptions, and examples—of practices and the projects of practices); debriefing interviews (sometimes using photographs for stimulated recall); field notes; open-ended or semi structured interviews; curriculum documents; audio- and video-records; precoded time spaced observation schedules (b) Micro interaction analysis, deductive thematic analysis, conversation analysis of talk-in-interaction, content analysis, document analysis, discourse analysis, historical analysis, interpretive phenomenological analysis, policy analysis
Finding doings in practice	*Material–economic arrangements* (in *physical space–time*)	(a) Participant and non-participant observation (what is done—the activities done in the physical space–time and material resources used at the time); interviews and focus groups (participants' accounts and interpretations of the activity); spatial maps (drawings of classrooms, consultation rooms or meeting spaces); copies of participant products or artefacts from the practice; photographs of the lay-out and physical set-ups; audio- and video-records; open-ended or semi structured interviews; precoded time spaced observation schedules (b) Micro interaction analysis, deductive thematic analysis, activity system analysis (actants, sequences, artefacts, etc.), interpretive phenomenological analysis, historical analysis

(continued)

Table 4.1 (continued)

Practices	Practice architectures	Accessed via (a) principal data gathering techniques and (b) analyses
Finding relatings in practice	*Social–political arrangements* (in *social space*)	(a) Observation (records of how people and things relate in the practice); interviews and focus groups (participants' accounts and interpretations of the interpersonal relationships and relational demands, expectations and experiences); field notes and audio- and video-records (e.g., noting and recording speaker-hearer, roles & relationships); spatial maps (showing proximity and positionality and movement of actors); open-ended or semi structured interviews; precoded time spaced observation schedules (b) Micro interaction analysis, deductive thematic analysis, conversation analysis, critical discourse analysis, policy analysis, interpretive phenomenological analysis, historical analysis

Adapted from Edwards-Groves and Grootenboer (2024)

outside the practice and influential practice architectures) must be applied to ensure rigorous and robust analysis. Additionally, it is important that the researcher avoids the pitfall of simply assigning a linear relationship between sayings and cultural–discursive arrangements, doings and material–economic, and relatings and social–political arrangements. Although these are intricately aligned, they are also interrelated and so not acknowledging this 'entanglement' makes for a conceptually benign application of the theory. For example, material–economic arrangements involving the physical set-ups in a classroom lesson space (e.g., desks in rows with a teacher at the front near the board), influences not only what activities can be done (the doings), but also how the people in the space (teachers and students) can relate to and interact with one another (the relatings).

4.2.1 Examples of Analytic Approaches

Typical of most qualitative methods, each approach involves systematically coding, decoding, and encoding the close multiple 'readings' of data generally represented in the form of texts (e.g., transcripts, written or visual records of field observations, written participant accounts, texts, or artefacts). Depending on the analytic method applied, these data are collated and assigned labels (codes, themes, or categories) to indicate the presence of coherence and interesting, prominent, and/or relevant content. In general terms, by systematically labelling the data (in terms of content, dimension, ecological relationships and interelateablity), researchers then analyse patterns of content by using qualitative methods that elicit meanings of content within the analytic texts produced (transcripts, codes, content maps, relational practice webs, etc.). Many researchers use multiple methods of practice analysis in their work as a more comprehensive way to examine and determine findings. Next, we present a brief outline of the some of the analytic methods we use in our own research.

4.2.1.1 Example 1—Practice Webs

To establish interelateablity between practices and as a form of historical tracing, some researchers connect these data visually though the production of concept maps or mind maps (see, e.g., Kemmis & Mutton, 2012; Kemmis et al., 2014; Mahon, 2014), we also describe these relational maps as *practice webs*. These can be developed as a *sayings web* (that explicates the complex of interconnections of discourses and language that prefigured and influence the practice), a *doings web* (that explicates the complex of interconnections of activities and materiality that prefigures and influences the practice), or a *relatings web* (that explicates the complex of interconnections of social relationships that prefigures and influences the practice), (see figure below as an example of a relatings web).

Prominent in the researcher's analytic activity is ensuring that the data gathered illustrates the extent to which practices are:

- *distributed* among participants at the time and over time (see Fig. 4.1 as an example of the distribution of practices concerning relatings between stakeholders and their activities like attending professional learning, completing courses, sourcing information form the library, being mentored, sharing the product of the practice—the ppt with Year 1 students),
- *orchestrated*, so that different people's contributions to a practice are integrated by a shared project—a common purpose (e.g., producing a customised animation in PowerPoint, Fig. 4.2),
- *enabled and/or constrained* by internal or external conditions (e.g., teacher access to literacy professional development, teacher and student knowledge of the customise function in PowerPoint, and their knowledge of the 'explanation' genre, teacher and student support offered by the district consultants and technology team, district office's literacy initiative),
- *understood* by practitioners present in terms of what is being said and done and the kinds of roles and relationships are evident (e.g., literacy instructional discourses, technology related discourses, deforestation texts and associated technical language, producing a multimodal text, Year 5's giving presentations to Year 1 students, teacher-student, Mrs C-teaching team, consultant-teacher),
- *internally diverse* or *differentiated*, so that they encompass different kinds of participants and differentiated kinds of contributions to the overall project of the practice (librarian-teacher, Year 5 peer group-Annie, Year 1 students-Year 5 students), and

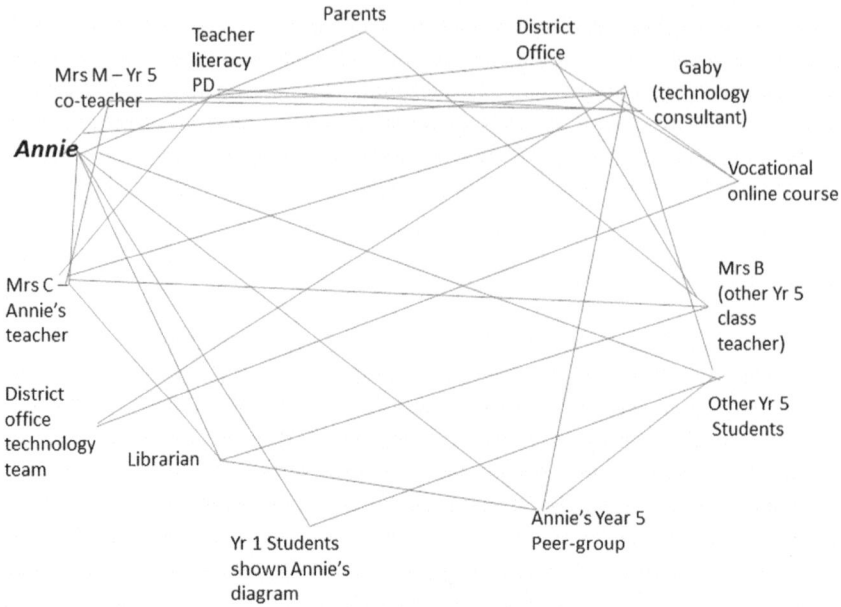

Fig. 4.1 Year 5 student Annie's web of interrelationships required for learning about and producing a customised animation in PowerPoint

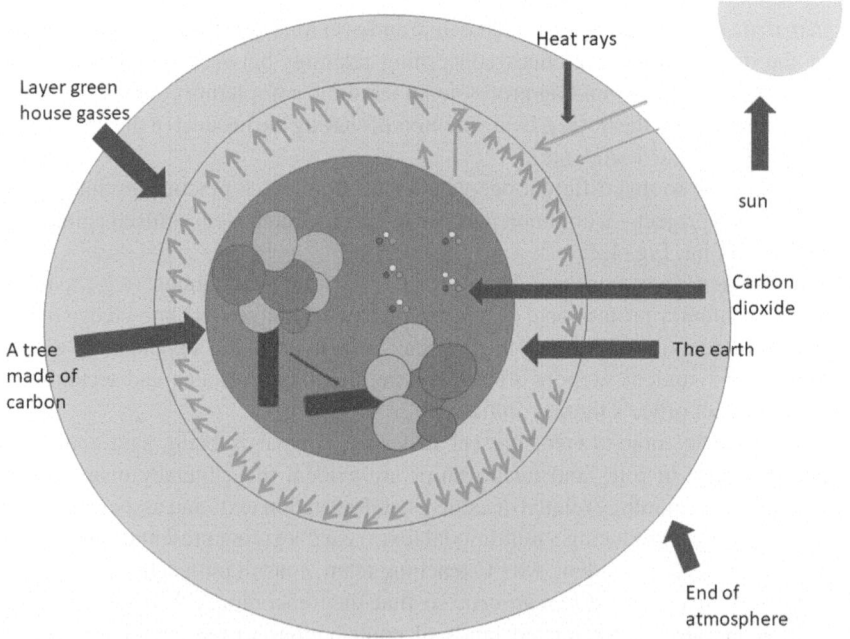

Fig. 4.2 Annie's moving diagram

4.2 Analysis of Practices

- *ecologically dependent on other practices* with which they connect, in the way that teaching practices, for example, may be dependent on practices of professional learning that shape or influence them (literacy professional development session informed teacher practices about explanation genres, district office technology team's participation in an online course).

4.2.1.2 Example 2—Transcript Analysis for Revealing Practices and Practice Architectures

Transcripts are a technology for analysis (Edwards-Groves, 2008, 2018). The preparation of transcripts for analysis is an important step in qualitative research, and indeed practice-based research. While transcription is one important way to *pin down* the talk and interaction so that it can be examined carefully (Edwards-Groves & Davidson, 2017, p. 35), there is no one way to develop a transcript, nor is there one definition or singular understanding (Davidson, 2009). However, approaching transcription requires applying a systematic approach, this is necessary for analytic efficacy. Notwithstanding the many challenges involved in 'turning' raw data in the form of spoken and observed actions into the words that comprise practices-in-action, or accounts of them as they are expressed in interviews, we begin this section with a brief outline of some steps we use in our own research.

Generally speaking, many people view a transcript to be the written representation of previously spoken words and actions that were done in practice; they are not data, but rather a mode for representing data. As Edwards-Groves and Freebody (2022, p. 78) stated, detailed transcript analysis of interactions provides

> ways that stay close-enough to the actual events that comprise those complex settings, and that provide sufficient detail and visible reportage, that the reader can engage, challenge, and critique researchers' interpretations and the implications of the findings.

Next, we give some steps that enable a systematic approach to encoding key features of verbatim talk and interactions recorded in observations of practices and interviews (based on the processes detailed by Edwards-Groves & Davidson, 2017, p. 35).

1. Play a little of the recording and write down as many words as you can hear.
2. Insert (   ) when you cannot yet hear words properly. Later you may be able to fill in these missing words.
3. Work your way through the recording in this way.
4. Play again, inserting more words. Again use (   ) to represent words that you cannot hear. Later, if there are words that you can't quite distinguish—put in your best guess using (*word/s*). You may alter these words at some stage, or your transcript may always signal that you have had a best guess at words that are hard to hear.
5. Now address *overlap* or *interruptions* in the talk. Ensure that you carefully show the exact place where beginnings of overlap occur. You may, or may not, wish to

show the end of overlaps. This is important for showing interactional roles and agency.
6. Then record timings and silences in turns and between turns (this is important since overlaps and gaps may indicate the relationships and levels of comfort interlocutors have in their practicing). These only need to be approximations but remember that tenths of seconds may be important for naturally occurring observations like a lesson or a meeting.
7. Add in other features of talk that you are interested in. For example, it may be that you want to show intonation or changes in pitch or other discourse patterns, or 'wait time' between turns, or questioning techniques.
8. Finally, number lines or turns so that you have a complete transcript for your analytic purposes. Your transcript should be presented clearly and carry the necessary information that align with your research interest.

Of course, it may be necessary to have the recordings transcribed professionally (particularly helpful for less complex interactions such as interviews); in this case you would maintain the integrity of the above listed steps, while perhaps not doing all the turn-by-turn transcribing yourself.

Since our ethnographic work often entails the collection of data yielding a large number of often extensive transcripts (especially when observing events like lessons, focus groups or meetings involving multiple parties), we accept it is neither profitable nor indeed possible to somehow present 'all' the relevant data. Because of this, transcript analyses often proceed along the following lines (adapted from Frieberg & Freebody, 1996, p. 188):

1. Make discerning selections of recorded observations of practices to develop initial word only transcripts (that may be subsequently developed into more comprehensive transcripts using, for instance, Jefferson notation system (2004) for preparing more fine-tuned, thematically focused transcripts; see also Edwards-Groves & Davidson, 2017, pp. 33–55 for a detailed account); it may be necessary to develop full transcripts of interviews or focus groups.
2. Scan the entire corpus to obtain a sense of the main features of the practice being studied.
3. Then guided by our research questions look for transcripts, or segments of transcripts or supplementary field notes, of the specific practice event or sections from across the larger study that particularly exemplify the features of interest.
4. Next, we attempt to explicate more precisely what the observable features involve in terms of the main concerns of the research; e.g., the nature of practices; the *in-situ* practice architectures evident.
5. We then re-examine the corpus of transcripts to check that our emerging definitions, descriptions and illustrations of the prevalent features (evident in the empirical material) are still faithful to our initial intuitions or sense of the features of the corpus.
6. After refining and cross-checking our descriptions and definitions of these features, we develop some tentative themes aimed at the production of findings and recommendations for change, and begin to compile a set of illustrative

4.2 Analysis of Practices

transcripts from corpus that show the features; checking that the examples can be read as clear examples of the feature or problem in question.
7. Finally, examples are selected for dissemination (for conferences and publications in reports, and/or journal articles) from the compilation of good examples of the features that informed the themes. In some cases, final selections are made because a particular section of transcript showed in a highly condensed way the feature in question. In other instances, the examples are included because they show a particular feature clearly disentangled from other practices, problems or patterns.

We generally operate on premises offered by Lee (1991), who in her ethnomethodological approach to study of social life, outlined five principles that characterise our approach to the analysis of practices; note, we add two additional principles (four and seven) below.

- The first is to suspend general questions such as relationships among gender, socioeconomic status, ethnicity, productivity, demographics, and achievement until those attributes of people and their activities have been translated in situ into courses of action that are *observable* and *understandable* by the participants setting being studied;
- second, treat social practices, such as sayings, doings and relatings, as jointly produced observable social events, rather than as products of, for example, knowledge, cognition or linguistic choices or the personality, disposition, or cultural attributes of people;
- third, explore, as an analytic aim, how the practitioners of practices (the people present at the time) evidently orient to one another as they co-ordinate their everyday courses of action in and through their interactions, relationships and activities;
- fourth, study the local discursivity of the talk in interaction as a practice unfolds over the duration of time the practice is being observed (which may, by the way, reveal hierarchies of power, instances of solidarity or individual and collective agency), without pre-empting what the structures of interactive routines might be expected to look like, rather than beginning with the conceptually yet-to-be analysed notions of language, work and power;
- fifth, treat the orderliness of culture as something that is achieved day-to-day in ordinary activities by people, and that therefore that orderliness can be revealed in the details of courses of their everyday action, rather than something that is given as a backdrop;
- sixth, think of culture, whether you want to use that in the big sense of the cultures of Australia or in the smaller sense of local sites such as the classroom culture, organisational culture, or the social culture of youth, as embedded in and built by courses of everyday action, because that is how members of our culture encounter it, rather than as something that is external to and constraining of practice in action. For instance, students do not encounter educational phenomena as abstract bureaucratic exigencies or as curriculum packages, or as ideas in the mind of a teacher as she plans her lessons. These are encountered as enlivened, mutually constructed

interactions, and as textual materials opening and closing opportunities to talk and lines of interpretation, and through the power differentials experienced teacher authority;
- seventh, in the analysis bracket your own interpretations, bias, attitudes and perceptions, and endeavour to let the data speak, so that the thematic points reveal themselves as evidence in the data.

Analysing transcripts can reveal how people (as interactive practitioners in practices) (e.g., teachers and students in their lessons, doctors and patients in their consultations, accountants and their clients in financial meetings) meet one another as interlocutors in sayings (informed by discourses and language), in the doing of activities and by relating to one another in different kinds of interpersonal relationships.

Transcript analysis of the activity of practice shows the distinctive and dynamic dimensions of practices as discursively produced, and how the flow of discursivity holds culture, language, activity, and social relationships together in a practice. These show how interaction works to influence participants consequential sayings, doings, and relatings as these unfold in the moment-by-moment interactions which occur in their activity. Furthermore, at a deeper level, examining transcripts reveals how practices are composed as interlocutory activities primarily concerned with intersubjective meaning making.

In the next example (from Edwards-Groves, 2018), a transcript analysis is linked with a table of invention to provide a more robust representation and comprehensive analytic approach to the study of the practice architectures of classroom lesson practices. Table 4.2 brings together an example of the constellation of practices and practice architectures that shape the conduct of pedagogical practices found in a lesson (evident in Extract 4.1, adapted from Edwards-Groves, 2018).

Table 4.2 Extract 4.1: Class discussion about the images in a book

20. T:	Don't call out, wait your turn Josie, be fair! We all get a say here,
21.	wait your turn. There's an animal in this picture, can you see it?
22. S(s):	[Yes::s] [Yes] [Yes]
23. S4:	[It's a lizard
24. T:	Can you see what it is?
25. S(s):	[Ye::es
26. Ben:	[no::o
27. T:	Why not Ben?
28. S(s):	((utterances called out from students))
29. Ben:	Cos its granite it's made out-it's made out of, like rock
30. T:	Do you think it's really made out of rock, Ben?
31. Ben:	[No, it's a thorny devil

As Table 4.2 coupled with the transcript extract illustrates, grasping the minute intricacies of the practices of teaching and learning requires understanding how the bundles of practice architectures arrange practices as they unfold discursively through language and sequences of time, in actions and interactions. In this classroom lesson example, these occur as a body or constellation of practices intertwined or enmeshed

4.2 Analysis of Practices

Table 4.2 Connection practice and practice architectures from a transcript to a table of invention

Practice architectures	Broader prefiguring practice architectures (examples)	Practices found in (or brought to) the lesson as a site of teaching and learning practice	Empirical examples from a lesson transcript (extract lines given) above
The cultural–discursive arrangements	The externally mandated national curriculum; the school's local policy outlining the integration of English with other disciplines like science; student's prior knowledge of local fauna (like wedgetail eagles, blue tongue lizards, the impact of feral animals on native fauna) and specific usage of technical terminology; teacher's knowledge of the student's rural background experiences; teacher's prior knowledge of science and English instruction	*Sayings* constituted by the discipline content or technical language of science which has particular meanings attributed to them in science	e.g., terra, terrarium (line 13); aquarium (line 14); camouflage (line 15); granite (line 29); thorny devil (line 31), moss (line 40); lichen (lines 42, 43); predators (line 47); wedgetail eagle (line 54)
		The language and discourse of the English curriculum which has particular meanings attributed to English instruction	e.g., getting ideas (line 1); rich vocabulary (line 10–11; a good metaphor (line 36); beautiful adjectives (line 57); expressive sentences (line 57–8); clear images in our minds (line 58); good discussion points (line 63); good information to build on and add (line 64)
The material–economic arrangements	Arrangements of desks in pod groups in the room; resources like books and computers are differently arranged in the English lesson as distinct from the science lesson to enable this particular reading activity to be 'done'; the teaching and learning resources available at the school; library resources; internet access and approved search engines; prior participation in science groups; prior participation in the science lesson on terrariums; teacher's prior knowledge of the kinds of activities and resources required for teaching reading, writing and science; student's knowledge of 'the way we do reading'	*Doings* shaped by particular activities forming this lesson phase like learning 'big words', having a whole class discussion, remembering and recalling	e.g., reading—have a bit of a read (line 1); getting ideas (line 1); revising—remembering and recalling vocabulary (lines 10); learning (line 11); answering teacher questions I am gonna ask you two in a minute (line 17); being more explicit (line 53); adding good discussion points (line 63); listen to each other (line 63), you all have such good information to build on and add (line 64)
		How the physical set-ups of material objects in the classroom space or how the students are positioned, seated or arranged in the space influence what is or can be done	e.g., get in a comfy spot on the floor (line 2); everyone facing front so you can see (line 2); sitting beside your talking buddies (line 3); seated in science groups (line 10); moving away from the bin (line 10); or on the floor or sitting next to their partner (line 11); seeing the picture on the cover of the book (line 17–8)

(continued)

Table 4.2 (continued)

Practice architectures	Broader prefiguring practice architectures (examples)	Practices found in (or brought to) the lesson as a site of teaching and learning practice	Empirical examples from a lesson transcript (extract lines given) above
The social–political arrangements	Teacher's prior knowledge of the students (interest, abilities and behaviours); teacher's pedagogical knowledge about the benefits of group work; the teacher's recent professional development about dialogic pedagogies; prior experiences of the interactional conduct and behaviour management of students in lessons, e.g., teachers nominating the next speaker, students complying with the teacher's requests	*Relatings* shaped by the ways teachers relate to their students would be different to how students would relate to their peers; students address the teacher in a formal way; following lesson rules	e.g., working in groups (line 11); like working with their partner (line 12); like being fair (line 20) and waiting your turn (line 21); we all get a say here (line 20); addressing the teacher appropriately Mrs. Kallo (line 19, 50); teacher asking for students' opinions, what do you think? (line 51); teacher calling for 'hands up' (line 58); or listening to others (line 63); no calling out (line 64)
		Positioning of students on the floor beside their 'talking buddy' but facing towards the teacher influences how they relate to others	Everyone facing front (line 3); sitting beside your talking buddies (line 3) or partner (line 12)

in the activity of discussing the content of a book in a reading lesson. Further, these simultaneously enable particular kinds of sayings, doings and relatings to exist or come to exist in the lessons at the moment of enactment. In other words, teaching and learning practices both constitute and are constituted by the particular words used (e.g., scientific terminology is required to make the lesson characteristically a science lesson or an English lesson), the particular activities done (e.g., the discussion that required students to recall the scientific terms encountered earlier) and the particular relationships which exist between the teachers and students present (e.g., as they listen to one another, comply with the teachers expectations). Added to this, the table shows ways practices are also influenced by other broader conditions (like the curriculum or a teacher's professional development programme) that may prefigure but not necessarily predetermine what actually happens in the discursively produced flow of lesson interactions (like the student's actual responses to a teacher question). These ideas are represented in the table as a means to collate, and show ways that lessons evolve in the moments of enactment and are influenced, but not predetermined by prefiguring conditions or practice architectures. A table such as this can be used to collate, organise and represent data gathered in a range of practice fields (in health and business).

4.2.1.3 Example 3: Interaction Analysis

Since practices generally involve multiple parties (for instance, groups of students in a classroom or a number of business partners at a monthly board meeting), the nature of their actual in-the-moment, turn-by-turn interactions, as they come together as interlocutors, forms an important part of practice-based research. Therefore, practice theorists often apply forms of interaction analysis to their transcripts of naturally occurring interactions (like in a lesson as represented in the transcript excerpt); this may include the use of more complex methods such as 'conversation analysis' (see Sacks et al., 1974). Interaction or conversation analysis focuses on the details of the discursive flow of turns that form the *interactions* among participants in their practices (Keyton, 2018; Sacks et al., 1974). Its importance to practice theory is explained here by Bonito and Sanders (2011, cited in Keyton, 2018, p. 10):

> Without close attention to the specifics of group members' conduct and interaction, it is easy for oversimple generalisations and unexamined assumptions to go unchecked, and to overlook that members' conduct and interaction is the basis for much that does not happen, as well as what does happen.

For the practice theorist, interaction analysis provides a systematic approach for coding and interpreting data about practices and the sites in which the observations occurred. This is important for explicitly revealing the sayings, doings, and relatings and ways interlocutors hear and understand the discourses, activities, and relationships as experienced in the practice being studied (See above section for detail on the preparation and analysis using transcripts).

Specifically, interaction analysis enables detailed understandings of human activity by capturing the sequential courses of action involved in the discursive flow of conversations that hold many practices together. It provides a systematic approach for studying how participants create intersubjective meanings or shared understandings, which subsequently influences their actions and understandings and ways of relating with one another (there and then). Analysis of recorded and transcribed in-situ conversations provides insights into the actual detailed work of interlocutors as they encounter one another in practices.

4.2.1.4 Example 4—Coding, Deductive Thematic Analysis and the Theory of Practice Architectures

Much of the research using the theory of practice architectures applies Fereday and Muir-Cochrane's (2006) *deductive thematic analysis*; a hybrid approach to Braun and Clarke's (2006) more commonly used thematic analysis. Deductive thematic analysis allows researchers to begin the process with a predetermined coding system (here, the dimensions of theory of practice architectures), but also offers scope for inductively updating and refining that coding system as new content is encountered during the process. Specifically, in studies using the theory of practice architectures, a framework that includes the practices (sayings, doings, and relatings), the practice architectures (cultural–discursive, material–economic, and social–political), along with dispositions and practice traditions are used as a preliminary organising framework to code and analyse data.

Researcher-imposed structures, like this, are placed on the data and used as an iterative, interpretive basis to explore those that are aligned with or confirmative of, or 'anomalous to, or disconfirming of the original data' (Freebody, 2003, p. 83). The process includes comparing, contrasting, corroborating, and legitimating findings as aligned with the framework and necessitates articulating discrepancies, and/or establishing gaps and mismatches between data sources. It involves a highly iterative and reflexive looping pattern of revisiting the data across multiple cycles (Berkowitz, 1997; Bruce, 2007) as additional questions emerge, new connections unearthed, and more complex formulations developed along with a deepening understanding of the material.

Drawing on Srivastava and Hopwood (2009, p. 74), each analytic cycle often involves approaching the data in terms of:

- explicitly engaging with current understandings related to the framework offered by the theory of practice architectures, and
- refining the focus and linking back to the research questions.

This approach is taken to complement the research aim by allowing the tenets of the social phenomenology to be integral to the process of deductive thematic analysis while allowing for new themes to emerge directly from the data using subsequently applied inductive coding (Fereday & Muir-Cochrane, 2006, p. 4). Here, researchers conduct continuous rounds of data interrogation in a summative reiterative-analytic step towards analytic reliability. As they approach data, and to guide their preliminary analysis researchers may ask themselves:

- What historical, ecological, and political traces of discourses (as cultural–discursive arrangements) are evident in the semantic space? In the happeningness? In participant accounts? In the artefacts (policy and other products of practices)?
- What historical, ecological, and political traces of materials, resources and physical set-ups (as material–economic arrangements) are evident in the physical space–time? In the happeningness? In participant accounts? In the artefacts (policy and other products of practices)?
- What historical, ecological, and political traces of particular relational configurations and hierarchies (as social–political arrangements) are evident in the social space? In the happeningness? In participant accounts? In the artefacts (policy and other products of practices)?

Applying a recursive process affords deeper insights about the practice architectures that characterise the practices (as experienced and perceived by practitioners) they are examining.

4.2.1.5 Example 5—A Table of Invention

As we previously have written (Edwards-Groves & Grootenboer, 2024), many users of the theory of practice architectures develop a *table of invention* as an interpretative analytical apparatus that organises data (transcripts and/or field notes) in terms of

4.2 Analysis of Practices

researcher interpretations of practices and practice architectures. This is generally related to the schematic frame of the three practice architectures: cultural–discursive, material–economic, and social–political arrangements (see Appendix 2 as an example of the organising framework). As explained by Kemmis et al. (2014, p. 224), a 'table of invention'[1] can be traced back to Aristotle's *Rhetoric* which provides a structure to organise data by populating the separate cells according to a predetermined a set of topics or viewing platforms. Researchers often use a table of invention as a mapping tool to isolate empirical examples of the theoretical concepts proposed in the theory of practice architectures, where they generally organise the cells in the table according to practices and their dialectical relationship with practice architectures. It involves:

- *recording researcher determinations* in a relatively systematic but repeated approach that identifies how a practice (being observed in the field) is composed (in terms of its sayings—words and ideas, doings—activities, and relatings—roles and relationships), its project, and sometimes the dispositions it requires and develops;
- *making evidence-informed judgements* supported by transcript excerpts of interviews and field observations about how the practice takes place in a particular practicescape;
- *tracing* the historical, political, and disciplinary threads of the practices in question;
- *delineating* in detailed ways that practices are furnished with resources found in or brought to the site (in terms of cultural–discursive, material–economic, and social–political arrangements), and as a moment in an unfolding practice as part of a tradition which shapes and is shaped by what is happening (at a particular moment in time); and
- *identifying the interdependence between practices and practice architectures* as they appear in practice-arrangement bundles.

Developing a 'table of invention' allows the researcher some flexibility in that they can add or delete cells depending on the focus of their research. A table of invention offers convenient organising tool that allows informed interpreters to engage with a range of evidence to arrive at interpretations of how practices are shaped by practice architectures, and how different practices relate to one another in ecologies of practices (Kemmis et al., 2014, p. 232). They can explore something as broad as the history of a practice (for instance, of education, medicine, or business organisation), or be as detailed as a single lesson, doctor–patient consultation, or end of financial year meeting with your accountant about your business's tax rebate. One can use such a table to analyse a vast teaching practice as related to social constructivist pedagogy, or as narrow as the exchanges between students and teachers in a classroom reading lesson. As Kemmis et al. (2014, p. 232) said:

---

[1] The most comprehensive description of analysing data using a 'table of invention' appears in *Changing practices, changing education*, (Kemmis et al., 2014, pp. 223–271).

> in relation to the theory of practice architectures, much in the process of doing these analyses depends on the researcher's judgement of the value and weight of different pieces of evidence, on drawing inferences from what we can see in the evidence to what cannot be seen, and making reasonable sense about how things must be for them to 'hang together' in the world so it appears to us in the ways it does.

Therefore, when analyses are made, it is possible to see how, in particular cases and in particular sites and at particular times, practices occur in relation to practice architectures, in practice-arrangement bundles, in which what can be said and done in the practice, and how people and things relate to one another in the practice shapes and is shaped by practice architectures. Yet, it may be impossible to access sufficient evidence about epochs or events on large scales, and thus the practice architectures table may not offer much assistance in making such an analysis. Kemmis et al. (2014) concede, however, that the extent to which the evidence is sufficient is also always a matter of judgement, noting 'that the practice architectures framework table is not a machine that spits out a reading of the world; it is merely a prompt for a certain way of making a reading of it. It is the analyst who makes the reading, not the table' (Kemmis et al., 2014, p. 227).

4.3 Conclusion

In this chapter, we have outlined some robust practices for analysing and interpreting data when employing the theory of practice architectures. We outlined methods typical of qualitative methods that generally involve systematically coding, decoding, and encoding data through close multiple 'readings' of data often represented in the form of texts (e.g., transcripts, written or visual records of field observations, written participant accounts, texts, or artefacts). While our aim in this book is to make the theory of practice architectures, and ways of researching practices, as clear and accessible as possible, yet analysing practices is not that simple. Nevertheless, the critical point for the practice theorist is to employ systematic approaches to data analysis—ones that allow the researcher to actually understand the practices involved, and the practice architectures that enable and constrain them. Perhaps, the key consideration here is to maintain a site ontological perspective, always giving precedence to the actual unfolding of practices in real time and space.

Appendix 1: Table of Invention: An Example of Cells (Kemmis et al., 2014, p. 226)

Elements of practices	Practice architectures in the site
	Practice landscape
Project In this cell, we describe what we take to be the *project* (or *telos* or purpose) of the practice we are studying, based on the evidence available (for example, the content of a transcript and other related observational, interview or documentary evidence available). When a participant sincerely answers the question 'What are you doing?', they describe the *project* of the practice (from their perspective).	In this cell, we describe how people and objects are differently enmeshed in the interactions (that is, in the activity-timespace) of the practice being studied. Different people and objects may be involved at different stages or in different episodes or in different aspects of the practice, and they may participate in different roles or from different perspectives. Some objects not apparently relevant to the activities (the ceiling, for example) may in fact play a role in enabling or constraining the practice and in this way be enmeshed in the activity-timespace of the practice.
Sayings	*Cultural-discursive arrangements*
Doings	*Material-economic arrangements*
Relatings	*Social-political arrangements*

In the cells on the left, we identify the principal *sayings*, *doings* and *relatings* that compose and 'hang together in' the *practices* under study; alongside these, on the right, we identify (respectively) the principal *cultural-discursive*, *material-economic* and *social-political arrangements* that are resources that make possible (*prefigure*) the sayings, doings and relatings we observe. In the analysis, we aim to identify at least the most significant proximal arrangements that shape the sayings, doings and relatings observed (things present in the site), and, where relevant, more distal conditions (like more widespread languages of policy or theory, more extensive material layouts, or wider sets of social relationships in or beyond organisations) that are significantly enmeshed in the practices under study. Together, the cells on the left describe the **practice** in terms of what is said and done and how people relate in it; together, the cells on the right describe the **practice architectures** that form the *niche* (on the model of an ecological niche) that permits the practice to survive in the site.

> **Dispositions (habitus)**
>
> In this cell, we describe what we take to be the most significant *dispositions* (or *habitus*) called on or developed in the principal participants as they participate in the practice. Bourdieu (1990) describes the *habitus* as a set of dispositions developed by a participant enacting a practice in cultural, material and social fields (for example); these dispositions are what give the participant the 'feel for the game' that makes it possible for them to act appropriately in the field. In our view, dispositions include knowledge, skills and values. *Knowledge* relates chiefly to the *sayings* and cultural-discursive resources (in language, in semantic space) present in or brought to the site; *skills* relate chiefly to the *doings* and material-economic resources (in activity and work, in physical space-time) at the site; and *values* relate chiefly to the *relatings* and social-political resources (in power and solidarity, in social space) at the site.
>
> **Practice traditions**
>
> In this part of the table, we comment on the *practice traditions* that appear to be in play, reproduced, or transformed in the practice. This sets the interactions that compose the practice against a longer history of practice, including at least the history of practice in the local site (for example, in terms of how the participants have acted and interacted as part of the practice in the site over previous days, months or years). Where relevant, we also comment on the practice interpreted against a broader history of this kind of practice (for example, how practice in a particular classroom might be an expression of a practice tradition like progressive education or a particular approach to literacy education).

References

Berkowitz, S. (1997). Analyzing qualitative data. In Frechtling J., Sharp L. (Eds.), *User-friendly handbook for mixed method evaluations*. Arlington, VA: Division of Research, Evaluation and Communication, National Science Foundation.

Bonito, J. A., & Sanders, R. E. (2011). The Existential Center of Small Groups: Member's Conduct and Interaction. *Small Group Research, 42*(3), 343–358.

Braun, V., & Clarke, V. (2006). Using thematic analysis in psychology. *Qualitative Research in Psychology, 3*(2), 77–101.

Bruce, C. D. (2007). Questions arising about emergence, data collection, and its interaction with analysis in a grounded theory study. *International Journal of Qualitative Methods, 6*(1).

Davidson, C. (2009). Transcription: Imperatives for Qualitative Research. *International Journal of Qualitative Methods, 8*, 35–62.

Edwards-Groves, C. (2008). The Praxis-Oriented Self: Continuing (self) education. In S. Kemmis & T. Smith (Eds.), *Enabling Praxis: Challenges for Education* (pp. 127–148). Sense Publisher.

Edwards-Groves, C. (2018). The Practice Architectures of Pedagogy: Conceptualising the Convergences between Sociality, Dialogue, Ontology and Temporality in Teaching Practices. Chapter 7 In O. B. Cavero & N. L. Calvet (Eds.), *New Pedagogical Challenges in the 21st Century: Contributions of Research in Education* (pp. 119–139). InTech Publishing.

Edwards-Groves, C., & Davidson, C. (2017). *Becoming a meaning maker: Talk and interaction in the dialogic classroom*. PETAA.

References

Edwards-Groves, C., & Freebody, P. (2022). Articulating their education: Interviewing primary years students on their literacy learning. Transitions in literacy and classroom interaction across the school years. In Jones, P.T., Matruglio, E. & Edwards-Groves, C. (Eds.), *Transition and continuity in school literacy development* (pp. 233–252). Bloomsbury Press.

Edwards-Groves, C., & Grootenboer, P. (2024). *Practice architectures*. Oxford University Press.

Edwards-Groves, C. & Hardy, I. (2013). "Well, that was an intellectual dialogue!": How a whole-school focus on improvement shifts the substantive nature of classroom talk. *English Teaching: Practice and Critique. 12* (2), 116–136.

Edwards-Groves, C. & Rönnerman, K. (2021). *Generative Leadership: Rescripting the promise of action research*. Springer.

Fereday, J., & Muir-Cochrane, E. (2006). Demonstrating rigor using thematic analysis: A hybrid approach of inductive and deductive coding and theme development. *International Journal of Qualitative Methods, 5*, 1–11.

Freebody, P. (2003). *Qualitative research in education: Interaction and practice*.

Frieberg, J. & Freebody, P. (1996). Analysing literacy events in classrooms and homes: Conversation—analytic approaches. In, P. Freebody & C. Ludwig (eds.), *Everyday Literacy Practices in and out of Schools in Low Socio—Economic Urban Communities,* Vol. 1 (p.185–369), Centre for Literacy Education Research, Brisbane.

Hardy, I., & Edwards-Groves, C. (2016). Historicising teachers' learning: A case study of productive professional practice. *Teachers and Teaching: Theory and Practice, 22*(4), 538–552.

Jefferson, G. (2004). Glossary of transcript symbols with an introduction. In G. Lerner (Ed.), *Conversation analysis: Studies from the first generation* (pp. 13–31). John Benjamins Publishing.

Kemmis, S., & Mutton, R. (2012). Education for sustainability (EfS): Practice and practice architectures. *Environmental Education Research, 18*(2), 187–207.

Kemmis, S., Wilkinson, J., Edwards-Groves, C., Hardy, I., Grootenboer, P., & Bristol, L. (2014). *Changing practices, changing education*. Springer.

Keyton, J. (2018). Interaction Analysis: An Introduction. In E. Brauner, M. Boos, & M. Kolbe (Eds.), *The Cambridge Handbook of Group Interaction Analysis* (pp. 3–19). Cambridge University Press.

Lee, J. (1991). Language and culture: The linguistic analysis of culture. In G. Button (Ed.), *Ethnomethodology and the human sciences*. Cambridge University Press.

Mahon, K. (2014). *Critical pedagogical praxis in higher education*. Charles Sturt University.

Nicolini, D. (2012). *Practice theory, work, & organisation: An introduction*. Oxford University Press.

Sacks, H., Schegloff, E., & Jefferson, G. (1974). A Simplest Systematics for the Organization of Turn-Taking for Conversation. *Language, 50*(4), 696–735.

Srivastava, P., & Hopwood, N. (2009). A practical iterative framework for qualitative data analysis. *International Journal of Qualitative Methods, 8*(1), 76–84.

Chapter 5
Reporting Practices: Research Dissemination for Transformation

Abstract This chapter addresses an important aspect of research—the dissemination of findings. Reporting practice-based research assists in sharpening understandings and developing deeper insights about the *significant and influential dimensions of practices* as they are experienced in different practicescapes. Since *practices have an indissoluble relationship with practice architectures,* the chapter highlights how researching practices demands close attention be made to examining *and* communicating the complexity of practices—amidst their commonplace, routine, or everyday happening. In this chapter, we argue that fundamental goal of dissemination is to facilitate or provoke transformation. Central to satisfying this transformative aspiration, is considering the critical role that reporting and disseminating research findings have for informing and influencing the theoretical, practical, and critical goals of the academy, particular practice fields or domains, and importantly, practitioner's practices.

In this final chapter, we return to the principal purposes of practice-based research. That is, to sharpen understandings and develop deeper insights about the *significant and influential dimensions of practices* as they are experienced in different practicescapes, for the fundamental goal of facilitating or provoking transformation. Central to satisfying this transformative aspiration is considering the critical role that reporting and disseminating research findings have for informing and influencing the theoretical, practical, and critical goals of the academy,[1] particular practice fields or domains,[2] and importantly, practitioner's practices.[3] Across the chapters of this book, we have attempted to describe and illustrate how the theory of practice architectures,

---

[1] Some researchers have written monographs disseminating their practice-based research that drew on the theory of practice architectures that usefully show how the conceptual resources are put to work for the academy, for a field or for practitioners. See for example, Edwards-Groves & Rönnerman, (2021), on action research and professional learning; Kemmis et al., (2014) on education complex of practices; Wilkinson (2021), on educational leadership.

[2] See, e.g., Francisco (2020), on learning in vocational education settings; Kemmis (2021), on everyday community practices.

[3] See for example, Grootenboer et al. (2021a, 2021b), on middle leadership in schools.

and its interdependent conceptual resources, provides a useful interpretative approach for exploring a range of phenomena of interest in different practice fields or domains with the aim of developing deeply comprehensive, even stereoscopical, perspectives of practices.

Schatzki (2010) similarly captures this intent, when he describes practice-based research as aimed at producing

> ... a type of account that (1) articulates or appropriates a conceptual framework that contains resources for capturing the actual multiplicity of human life, and (2) formulates a variety of significant propositions that hold universally, generally or of particular collections of lives. (p. xvi)

He continued, saying that any investigation of practices.

> ... aims to articulate an abstract, general framework about activity, society, and history that both captures universal and general truths about actual human existence and can inform investigations of particular activities, social formations, and historical phenomena. (pp. xvi–xvii)

Yet, at the same time, we are acutely aware that generalised abstractions alone negate the critical specificity and particularity that site-based research affords. Noting we also recognise that there is always a measure of abstraction and interpretation in reporting research findings.

As a point of review, a site ontological approach to the study of practices means being attuned to the notion that practices are shaped by the sites in which they occur, and that, reciprocally, social sites are shaped by the practices that occur in them. This means that we cannot study practices without looking at, and showing, the intricate and nuanced ways practices are conditioned by the sites in which they happen; and we can't study social sites without seeing, and illustrating, how they have been shaped by the practices that happen in them at a particular moment in time. Here, the site ontological perspective thus allows us to see, and report, *how* every site is unique, *how* every practice is unique, and *how* practices are remade anew on each occasion of practicing. Thus, it forces us to stop thinking about practices like teaching or learning, consulting, or meeting *in generalised abstractions*, and start thinking about how they are unique, in all their *particularity* (Kemmis & Edwards-Groves, 2018).

Capturing the reciprocity between the abstract or esoteric notions of human sociality and the nuanced site-based specificity and particularity of practices is an idea which figures prominently in Schatzki's (2002) three senses of the site and encapsulated by our concept of the practicescape (explained in Chap. 3). In response, the site ontological interest of the theory of practice architectures draws its attention recursively from the site outwards and back in a dynamic interplay between sites, practices, and practice architectures. In our own research, we have been persistent in attention given to articulating and communicating the dynamism between the site-based happeningness of practices and their consequences, the interrelatedness between practices as captured by the notions of practice arrangement bundles and ecologies of practices, and showing ways that different analytic methods provide insights into characterising the nature and nuances of practices and practice architectures with varying degrees of intent and granularity. We see these as forming the critical task for reporting practices.

With these ideas in mind, in this chapter we turn specifically to reporting and disseminating new insights in terms of their role and impact in bringing about transformation to theory, methodology, politics, and practice. The first section addresses with dealing with articulating and communicating the complexity of practice.

5.1 Navigating the Complexities for Presenting Coherent Portrayals of Practices: Untangling the Problem of Practice

As we have found, presenting a coherent sense of the complexity of practices is not a seamless nor straightforward task, since by their very nature, practices happen amidst practice architectures in different practicescapes. So, comprehensibly and accessibly capturing the inherent complexity, tensions, ambiguities, and contradictions found in practice-based research are not without issues for the researcher. To tackle the challenges associated with this important research task, we begin first by reemphasising what we see as four key theoretical premises of the theory of practice architectures that act as both a filter and barometer for our own writing.

i. Since practices have an indissoluble relationship with practice architectures, to speak of practices means to speak of their intricate entanglement with practice architectures; and thus, consequentially as an implication, to transform practices necessitates transforming the practice architectures. Simply said, practices cannot be understood, reproduced, or transformed—and thus explained, without attention be given to the practice architectures, and vice versa.

ii. Practices are never neutral, are always prefigured (although not pre-determined), are always mediated and contested in their happening (by site-based conditions, other practices and practice architectures), are always enabled and constrained, and are always situated, thus nuanced and experienced locally.

iii. The three 'dimensions' of intersubjective space—evident as language in sayings appearing in semantic space and shaped by cultural–discursive arrangements, evident as activity in doings appearing in physical space–time and influenced by material–economic arrangements, and evident as relationships in ways of relating appearing in social space and influenced by social–political arrangements—are analytically distinct but always empirically intertwined.

iv. The theory of practice architectures is a social theory, and so a key interest is in reporting how practices are socially accomplished amidst enabling and constraining conditions. This exercise means not neglecting the role of practitioners of practices—those participating as interlocutors in practices and the intersubjective sensemaking required of them, since what is evident in their language, activity, and relationships (i.e., explicitly displayed in their sayings, doings and relatings) shows their comprehensibility of the situation—this must be accounted for.

With this in mind, communicating (writing and articulating) findings that draw from the conceptual resources framing the theory of practice architectures must take full account of these ideas and the relationship between them, demanding that they are described, explained, illustrated, and exemplified with evidence.

5.1.1 Capturing Analytic Distinctions Amidst Empirical Cohesion

To be faithful to the conceptual resources comprising the theory of practice architectures requires acknowledging the density of practices. Therefore, a central aim of reporting practice-based research, is to make the knotty problems of practice accessible to the field. Acknowledge, at the outset, that the distinctions made between practices and practice architectures (and their constituent features) are only drawn apart for analytic purposes, whilst noting the logical sense of coherence in the empirical realities of a practice (Gherardi, 2012). It is an empirical matter as to what extent practices, as a part of a site, are experienced in a way that is meaningfully understood by those present (e.g., teachers and students in classroom lessons, doctors and patients in medical consultations, or accountants and clients in their financial review meetings). This means examining, and then revealing, how sayings, doings and relatings in the discursive temporal flow of activity, 'display' the extent to which intersubjective meaning making is both possible and achieved, and enabled and constrained by practice architectures. Illustrating the inherent interplay between enablements and constraints is an important task for communicating the existential realities and site ontological conditions that bear down on how practices happen, where on any occasion of practicing some things are enabled and constrained at the same time.

Therefore, the task of reporting practices through the lens of the theory of practice architectures must be approached:

- empirically or descriptively in relation to showing the observable 'occasioned evidence' discovered about practices and the sites where they happen, and how people involved in practices orient to one another semantically in their sayings, in physical space–time in their doings, and socially in their relatings; for example, drawing on analysis of actual naturally occurring episodes of practice encountered in ethnographic observations or through the analysis of transcripts of audio or video records of practices as they unfold in real time;
- interpretively in relation to illustrating how the people involved in practices account for understandings about what they were doing and their perceptions about what enables and constrains their practices, and consequently, how we understand them as analysts; for example, drawing on analysis of interviews with people involved and affected by particular practices, as well as various kinds of document analysis; and,

- critically in relation to the discerning the paradoxes, ambiguities, injustices, stability, or sustainability of the practices of interest to derive evidence-informed implications for the development of different practice fields or domains; for example, drawing on systematic analysis and researcher judgements about evidence against an analytic framework related to mapping the interelateablity between criteria concerning, for instance, the coherence of ideas, the ways resources are used, and the moral, political and relational orders that may (or may not) justify what is done (adapted from Kemmis & Edwards-Groves, 2018; and Kemmis et al., 2017*)*.

As pointed out by Kemmis et al., (2017, p. 243), 'the point of the theory of practice architectures, then, is not to say merely that practices are shaped by practice architectures, or, merely that practice architectures are frequently shaped by practices'. Rather, its intent is to reach through, and beyond, these reciprocal relationships to arrive at critical insights about how practices and the practice architectures that make them possible are sustainable or unsustainable, just or unjust, reasonable or unreasonable, defensible or indefensible. For the researcher, 'this task involves making and reporting on all three of these kinds of analysis' (Kemmis et al., 2017, p. 243). One way this can be done, is first, to look at the phenomena of interest through each conceptual resource of the theory like a lens or a piece of a puzzle to examine its component parts. Then second, reassemble them so each can be seen in relation to the others, and in relation to the three senses of the site; for example, to see how the particular sayings, doings, and relatings of practices are shaped by, and shape, cultural–discursive, material–economic, and social–political arrangements, incorporating seeing how the practices are ecologically interdependent and historically prefigured.

To exemplify some of the ideas we have proposed about reporting practice-based research, we present a comprehensive case from a published book chapter (Edwards-Groves, 2018, *The practice architectures of pedagogy*) to illustrate the inter-relatability between data, analysis, dissemination, and the conceptual resources of the theory of practice architectures (see Example 5.1 below). The ideas can be usefully applied/translated to other practice fields.

5.1.2 Example 5.1

From drawing on analysis of video-recorded then transcribed classroom lessons, Edwards-Groves (2018) put the conceptual resources of the theory of practice architectures to work in this way. First, Edwards-Groves (2018, p. 122) introduced the practice site (end of a Year 3 lesson), then the project of the practice (recalling facts and terms from the science lesson) like this:

> *As an example, consider this short extract from the summary phase of a Year 3 lesson where the teacher is facilitating student recall of particular facts and terms arising from the earlier science lesson.*

Second, to show the practice architectures and practices of pedagogy, she used transcript excerpts from a lesson (Extract 1 below, adapted from Edwards-Groves, 2018, p. 122) as empirical data to show how the practices unfolded in interaction between interlocutors (here the teacher and the year 3 students in a class discussion).

Extract 1: Pedagogy in practice

1.	Sam: it's dirt, terra is dirt
2.	T: dirt, yes Sam, terra means dirt or earth, so:o aqua is water and terra is earth
3	so we've got our little container [with earth-and what's that, Josh?
4.	Josh: [a terrarium
5.	Sally:it's got to have a top on top of it, a lid to make it work
6.	T: mm Josh excellent, terrarium, the technical term (pause) yes a lid, it's gotta
7	have a lid on it (pause) right, okay tell me more Sally, listening everyone
8.	Sally: to keep the moisture in
9.	Shay: ha to keep our blue tongue ((lizard)) in
11.	Ss: ((laughter))
12	T: yes Shay, Bluey is an escape artist you're right about that (pause) well that's
13	enough discussion about ah terrariums…

Third, following the data excerpt, to introduce her analysis of the lesson practices, she drew on a range of relevant concepts (such happens, practice, unfolds discursively, sociality, interlocutors), writing:

> As the lesson happens, it unfolds discursively through moments of time, in moments of sociality, with each turn in an interaction following the next to form the discussion about terrariums. By reading through the transcript, it becomes clear that the concept of pedagogy— and the teaching and learning practices that comprise it—cannot be understood without accounting for the social. Here, the sociality of pedagogical practice is evidenced since to 'get this lesson done' these students and their teachers interact with one another in the lesson as interlocutors co-participating in instructional dialogues about terrariums and aquariums. In this sense, pedagogy is characteristically social. (2018, p. 123)

Fourth, as Edwards-Groves continued, she identified *and* exemplified the particular site-specific sayings, doings, and relatings as pertaining to the particular occasion of practicing—that science lesson at that time, that she was using as representative data in the publication:

> It is evident that in this Year 3 Science lesson, participants (the students and their teacher) enact:
>
> 1. characteristic or particular *sayings* formed discursively in language known to and spoken by those present (like using specific scientific terms and language such as terra, aqua, terrarium, earth, moisture, blue tongued lizard; see for e.g., lines 1, 2, 3, 4, 6, 8 & 9),
>
> 2. characteristic or particular *doings* formed through doing activities understood and undertaken by those present (like reading a book, writing, engaging in a class discussion; see for e.g., lines 1–10), and
>
> 3. characteristic or particular ways of *relatings* developed through the ways these students and their teacher related to one another in their different roles and understood relationships they demonstrate there (like peers in a cohort, or a teacher with power over students). (2018, p. 123)

5.1 Navigating the Complexities for Presenting Coherent Portrayals ...

Fifth, notions of the interconnectedness between practices were drawn together in relation to this project (the science lesson about terrariums), as connected to how practices unfold in 'real time flows of time'. Here she also emphasised the importance of a site ontological view of pedagogy by highlighting and illustrating the specificity of this concept as exemplified in the empirical material presented. Edwards-Groves (2018, p. 124) wrote:

> These characteristic sayings, doings and relatings are tightly entangled and interconnected in ways that formed for them this distinctive project, this particular 'lesson' about terrariums. These three dimensions of the practice of pedagogy unfold discursively through language in real flows of time as characteristically interdependent and overlapping. However, this is far too simple a view of practices since it overlooks the particularity of the conditions and circumstances that exist in the actual site itself. For example, the particular students in this particular Year 3 classroom knew about blue tongue lizards because their local experience of them enabled them to bring this knowledge into this practice (evidenced in lines 8–10), or that the use of technical terminology is valued and praiseworthy (see line 6).

Sixth, to conclude this section of analysis in the chapter, Edwards-Groves (2018, p. 131) drew out the influential conditions that might have 'prefigured' what happened, and then specified ways that the practices of the particular lesson were *interwoven* (or *enmeshed* according to Schatzki or as Hodder suggested *entangled*) with sites, not just 'set' in them.

> In lessons, these occur as a body or constellation of practices intertwined or enmeshed in the doing; and further simultaneously enable particular kinds of sayings, doings and relatings to exist or come to exist in classroom lessons at the moment of enactment. In other words, teaching and learning practices in classrooms both constitute and are constituted by the particular words used (scientific terminology is required to make the lesson characteristically a science lesson or an English lesson), the particular activities done (like the discussion that required students to recall the scientific terms encountered earlier) and the particular relationships which exist between the teachers and students present as they listen to one another, comply with the teachers expectations. But added to this, practices are also influenced by other conditions (like the curriculum or a teacher's professional development program) that may prefigure but not necessarily predetermine what actually happens in the discursively produced low of lesson interactions (like the student's actual responses to a teacher question). This means that pedagogy in the moments of enactment is influenced, but not predetermined by prefiguring conditions or practice architectures.

5.1.3 *Implementing an Impactful Transformative Dissemination Strategy*

Disseminating research findings is an essential step towards development and change in any field of study. Designing and implementing a dissemination or reporting strategy, regardless of media, is fundamental for increasing the visibility of research findings, attracting public engagement in the social sciences, instilling the confidence of society in research, and raising the possibilities for transformation. *Thus,* at its core, communicating research findings involves a designing a robust implementation strategy which recognises that

1. the procedures of distillation (i.e., the analyses and the bridge they form between the event and conclusions drawn from its study) are publicly accessible and this can be evaluated as publicly 'knowable' and 'trustable'; and
2. the findings are disseminated in some way to the range of stakeholders in the [relevant] field or domain, for information, for scrutiny and for challenge, and they are disseminated in ways that afford [and elicit] scrutiny and challenge (Freebody, 2003, p. 28).

In general terms, disseminating research findings requires different kinds of literacies which enables researchers to effectively, and succinctly, summarise, publicise, and so mobilise their central ideas. Publicly sharing work may involve a range of modes whether it be publishing a journal paper or making conference presentations to the academy or seminars with stakeholder groups; or through other innovative media including using blogs, tweets, podcasts (e.g., *A World Worth Living In • A podcast on Spotify for Podcasters*) and social media to increase reach and promote interest. It might mean making use of press releases and infographics, showcasing findings through stakeholder websites (where digital curation of information be stored), and/ or utilising interest groups as strategic alliances for dissemination. And depending on the project, filmmaking can also be a creative method of research dissemination (see, e.g., the PEP International World Worth Living In research project *Education for a World Worth Living In—Monash Education*).

5.1.3.1 Dissemination and Knowledge

Impacting the field of study is a key goal of research, one that aims to transform practices by contributing new insights and new knowledge. Dissemination has a dynamic relationship with knowledge creation but focuses on the communication, rather than the creation, of ideas, where communicating new knowledge involves both sense making and sense giving (Norris, 2022). However, understanding that from a practice perspective, 'knowledge arises from, represents, recalls, and returns to its use in practices' (Kemmis & Edwards-Groves, 2018, p. 116), forming a useful way for thinking of knowledge '*not* as the property of individual minds—individual cognitive subjects—but as something shared intersubjectively in practices' (Kemmis & Edwards-Groves, 2018, p. 118). This practice view of knowledge has implications for understanding the relationship between dissemination, knowledge, and transformation.

After Kemmis and Edwards-Groves (2018), we suggest that (new) knowledge about practices and practice architectures *arises from* the examining the practices in a particular community in a particular field; it comes from observing what people do, and how they live. Drawing on our running example of accountancy, knowledge about accounting, for example, *arises from* the observation and experience of people involved with business and finance: accountants, economists, business owners, clients, tax payers, administration officers, actuaries, marketeers, and many more. The knowledge of these people is represented in some form in their own thinking and neural pathways, but it is also represented in more public form in words, languages, specialist discourses, diagrams, book keeping programs, mathematical formulae, and other forms of texts about different facets of accountancy. Once represented, in minds or in texts, this knowledge recalls not only particular moments of individual people's experience, but also histories of business organisation, book keeping, government economic policy, auditing and annual taxation practices, accountancy software packages, and the specialised work of a variety of accountants and other related professionals. And, finally, this knowledge returns to its use in the practice of accountancy—whether auditing a new client, preparing tax returns for regular clients, or installing a new accountancy software program for a new business. Therefore, in a research sense, dissemination of (new) knowledge (about accountancy practices for example) can be said to be transformative, when evidence empirically shows traces of *how* and *that* the knowledge arises from, is represented, recalls, and returns to its use in (new) practices transformed by that new knowledge (Grootenboer et al., 2021a).

5.1.4 The Theory of Practice Architectures: Research for Transformation

In an effort to move beyond the status quo to 'transcend the 'givenness' of the world' so as to create 'alternative futures' (Stetsenko, 2014, p. 196), research for transformation is a critical imperative for practice-based research. Transformations are made possible when research findings meet and are taken up by the field—the academy, the field or domain, the site. It is in interpreting and critiquing practices—even the mundane, taken-for-grantedness, ordinariness or even the obscurity of practices, that steps can be taken to change—so transform—practices and practice architectures. On this, as Kemmis, Wilkinson, and Edwards-Groves (2017, p. 254) remind us that the theory of practice architectures.

> was devised to help us explore practices critically: to see when and how they were formed, reproduced, and transformed; what social conditions (practice architectures) make them possible and hold them in place; and how both practices and practice architectures might need to be changed if they turn out to have untoward consequences: if they are incoherent or unreasonable; wasteful, destructive, or unsustainable; or the cause of suffering or injustice.

With this in mind, practice-based research studies are often about site-based practice development (hence why the theory of practice architectures provides useful analytical tools for action research). As noted previously in this chapter, and in the preceding chapters, the theory of practice architectures is a critical theory that seeks not just to describe or understand practices, practice architectures, and practicescapes (although this is a common starting point)—it is about developing and transforming them, in that place and at that time (Grootenboer, 2018). So the reporting and dissemination of practice-based studies can serve to both show and understand how site-based practice development occurred in a particular site and provide a reflective touchstone for others as they consider the particular practices in their own practicescape or site (but not a recipe or prescription for how practices can be developed in another place at another time).

As suggested in previous chapters, the attention to the formation, the reproduction, and transformation of practices requires an evidence base (generally capturing and representing the actuality, artefacts and person accounts of practices) that explicitly illuminates the historical traces, ecological interconnectedness, and site ontological conditions which enable and constrain how practices are formed, reproduced, and transformed in the broad expanse of fields of interest to practice theorists. With this in mind, this chapter sought to show how dissemination for transformation can be facilitated by the theory of practice architectures.

5.1.4.1 Bringing the Threads Together: A Practice-Based *Re*turn to Researching Practices

Understanding practices also means understanding research as practice. This means understanding the practices and practice architectures of research scholarship. This view prompts us to attend to the sociality of phenomena critical to researching practice, its development and its advancement. This chapter entered this territory by considering ways that reporting, coproducing, and sharing research products, engagement in research activities and dissemination of research findings form academic practices with, within, and across the academy and different practice fields. The extent to which the different modes of dissemination are experienced and embedded in the practices of research is inscribed by empirical cases that establish the possibilities, benefits, and challenges concerned with 'researching practices in a site ontological way'. Thus, across the chapter, and indeed this book, an interesting but complex web of conceptual ideas are presented which bring into view two critical but intertwined principles for practice-based research: the nexus between practice-for-researching and researching-as-practice. These principles orient to the multidimensionality of particular forms of research practices that are fundamental for also engaging in a range of participatory approaches for reporting, engagement, and dissemination. The result of this conceptualisation is an insightful grasp of what must occur for practice-based research to realise its promise—to impact practices in a range of fields of interest in tangible, jointly constructed, accessible, and mutually understood practices.

Here we draw on the theory of practice architectures to consider the nature of practice-based research methods and the practices by which it is constituted in practice itself. This theory takes a social view of research which focuses attention on the particularity and distinctiveness of how researching practices happen in actuality (Kemmis et al., 2014). Considering researching practices from a social practice theory perspective helps us to understand practical, critical and theoretical ideas forming practice-focused questions and research design—this is simply so, since research itself influences and is influenced by arrangements that enable and constrain the very practices that underpin the conduct of research.

5.1 Navigating the Complexities for Presenting Coherent Portrayals …

We place virtue on how practice, in all its forms, is influenced by arrangements made apparent in semantic spaces, physical space–time, and social spaces for practitioners (researchers and practitioners alike) to partner as interlocutors in their endeavour to develop, contribute to, comprehend and advance practices experienced in actual sites of practice, both locally and at a distance (through a range of publication modes). Each of these spaces creates reciprocally influential conditions and resources for the other, and considered together, open up communicative spaces for communicative action (Habermas, 1987), and ideally, transformation. Here the remit for research is to create open and necessarily dialogic spaces that have the potential to produce research that is relevant, accessible, shareable and generative for those in the professions. As Kemmis et al. (2014) argue, opening up these spaces forms the basis of a practice turn for understanding and developing research practices that hang together cohesively; and as the authors acknowledge, ones that account for and achieve wide-reaching impact on both practice and policy. It is in this space that transformation is possible.

A practice *re*turn, as accounted for in the theory of practice architectures, recognises how a shared semantic space opens up the particular cultural–discursive arrangements that shape how meanings between interlocutors are negotiated and carried comprehensively to varying degrees through a range of dissemination practices. In this chapter, we described a few reporting practices that enable practitioners to make sense of one another as they report, engage with and disseminate research. For example, we highlighted reporting practices that are necessary for questioning, elaborating, reflecting, offering new perspectives on what has already been published and understood about a given topic, exchanging tacit knowledge, reasoning together about research evidence, coconstructing new knowledge, or building intermediate theories of practice. Taken together research for transformation is generated.

Considering research practices in semantic space means relating to what is done in the shared physical space–time is understandable among those who encounter research through a range of dissemination modes. Here the conduct of research is responsive to material–economic arrangements that impact the time, distances, material resources, and physical setups found in particular research activities themselves. In practice, these are never seamless and always contested as they simultaneously influence and are influenced by the particular circumstances and needs of research practitioners (including the researcher and the research participants) in the particular research practices, that are conducted in specific contexts and who are practising their research under particular conditions. For instance, activities such as engaging with published research, reading other people's work, coproducing research-based resource materials, different forms of writing, attending conferences, workshops or professional learning sessions, academic study, using research products and outputs, jointly analysing or reflexively critiquing videos of practices from different research domains. In many ways it was in engaging in such activities that the theory of practice architectures developed in the first place. To be productive and transformative, there is a need to account for different research reporting practices—including considering the research products and resources, and the physical setups for data gathering and dissemination like working in online environments, or in interviews and meetings, or seminars, workshops and conferences, or focus groups, or dialogue conferences and research circles, or working as coresearchers from different international contexts.

At the same time, semantic space and physical space–time are reciprocally and ecologically connected to social space where research practices are enabled and constrained by social–political arrangements (Kemmis et al., 2012, 2014). Importantly, practice-oriented researchers also need to take seriously the need to attend to the inevitable imbalance of power in research (between the researcher and the researched), and potential to shifting towards facilitating a more agentic and active position among practitioners and researchers. In social space, practice-oriented researchers and their participants may come to relate to one another more equitably, in solidarity and with agency as they participate in research partnerships, coinquiries, collaborations, jointly constructed projects and shared decision making as activist professionals within a community of critical inquirers (see Edwards-Groves, 2023, as an example, and Sachs, 2003). The forms of engagement suggested involves creating avenues for participants and researchers to respond to one another in open communicative spaces as they critique, report, analyse, engage with, and disseminate research (see Edwards-Groves & Davidson, 2017 critical participatory action research as an example). Moreover, these responses, enacted in practices, create interdependent conditions and preconditions that form practice architectures (Kemmis et al., 2014) that simultaneously influence both what happens in moments of practising (here researching) and what prefigures (although not necessarily predetermines) future researching practices. Spaces for, and practices of, research form conditions that ground and legitimise research activity in a way that moves practitioners from consumers to coproducers—thus creating opportunities for generating a transformative activist stance (Stetsenko, 2014).

We acknowledge that a practice-oriented position has the potential to capitalise on practitioners having equitable opportunities for exercising collective responsibility, and even accountability, for theory and knowledge building, and ultimately having agency and influence on and in the profession of which they are part (especially through approaches such as action research). The practice standpoint in research essentialises the need for 'people learn how to think together…in which the thoughts, emotions and resulting actions belong not to one individual, but to all of them together' (Isaacs, 1994, p. 358). As recognised, dissemination practices involve a three-way communicative condition of interlocutory meaning making shared between the researcher, research participants and research recipients—where nestled in this communicative space are transformative possibilities for all. Importantly, this becomes an emancipatory position located not in parallel to but enmeshed within the work of the academy. Consequently, as indicated by practice theorists across the globe, including our own work, research findings must return to the practice domain from which it emerged. This is a position of shared responsibility which breaks down more traditional boundaries and imbalances of power between researchers and practitioners to open up dialogic spaces for intersubjectivity or 'sensemaking interactions' between stakeholders at all levels—from researchers to policy makers to educators, healthcare workers or business managers (to use our rolling examples). This is at once, a critical moral and ethical repositioning.

Despite transformational aspirations of research on practices, reporting, engagement in and dissemination of research is often left constrained by circulating with the comforts of the academy. Against this tendency however, the practice position reflected in this chapter throws open the spaces and practices of research for collective and shared involvement, responsibility, and critique. This forms an invitation to all stakeholders to enter into dialogues with one another about what matters to them—practice transformation.

5.2 Conclusion

This chapter is but a brief foray into a complex series of issues concerning the role of reporting and communicating research findings for transformation. Indeed, given that reporting and dissemination are themselves practices, enabled and constrained by particular local practice architectures, they are also 'site specific'—in other words, there is no formula or 'best practice approach' for reporting research. However, here we have sought to highlight how moving from analysis to dissemination is a critical step in the shift towards transforming practices. The theory of practice architectures offers a multifocal lens to capture and examine the detail and complexity of practices, where the researcher is invited to draw on each of the theory's conceptual resources like a lens that guides the observation, interpretation, and dissemination. Yet, as we have proposed throughout the book, focusing on the minutia (e.g., the sayings, doings, and relatings) alone understates even minimises, the comprehensive existential conditions, and site ontological reality of practices. Since *practices have an indissoluble relationship with practice architectures,* researching practices demands close attention be made to examining and communicating the complexity of practices—amidst their commonplace, routine, or everyday happening, through examining their constitutive parts, yet not neglecting its comprehensive whole, nor its consequences or the enabling and constraining conditions. This is the ultimate challenge for the practice theorist—bring comprehensibility to the complexity that is practice.

References

Edwards-Groves, C. (2018). The practice architectures of pedagogy: Conceptualising the convergences between sociality, dialogue, ontology and temporality in teaching practices. In O. B. Cavero & N. L. Calvet (Eds.), *New pedagogical challenges in the 21st century: Contributions of research in education* (pp. 119–139). InTech Publishing.

Edwards-Groves, C. (2023). Sands through my fingers: Finding aboriginal cultural voice, identity and agency on Country. In K. Reimer, M. Kaukko, S. Windsor, K. Mahon, & S. Kemmis (Eds), *Living well in a world worth living in: Current practices of social justice, sustainability and wellbeing* (Vol 1, pp. 87–114). Springer.

Edwards-Groves, C., & Davidson, C. (2017). *Becoming a meaning maker*. Primary English Teachers Association Australia.
Edwards-Groves, C., & Rönnerman, K. (2021). *Generative leadership: Rescripting the promise of action research*. Springer.
Francisco, S. (2020). *Supporting the workplace learning of vocational and further education teachers: Mentoring and beyond*. Routledge.
Freebody, P. (2003). *Qualitative research in education: Interaction and practice*. Sage.
Gherardi, S. (2012). *How to conduct a practice-based study: Problems and methods*. Edward Elgar.
Grootenboer, P. (2018). *The practices of school middle leadership: Leading professional learning*. Springer.
Grootenboer, P., Edwards-Groves, C., & Kemmis, S. (2021a). A curriculum of mathematical practices. *Pedagogy, Culture and Society*. https://doi.org/10.1080/14681366.2021.1937678
Grootenboer, P., Edwards-Groves, C., & Rönnerman, K. (2021). *Middle leadership in schools: A practical guide for leading learning*. Routledge.
Habermas, J. (1987). *Theory of Communicative Action* (Vol. 2). Cambridge Polity Press.
Isaacs, W. (1994). Dialogue. In P. M. Senge, A. Kleiner, C. Roberts, R. B. Ross, & B. J. Smith (Eds.), *The fifth discipline fieldbook* (pp. 357–364). Nicholas Brealey.
Kemmis, S. (2021). *A practice sensibility: An invitation to the theory of practice architectures*. Springer.
Kemmis, S., & Edwards-Groves, C. (2018). *Understanding education: History, politics, practice*. Springer.
Kemmis, S., Edwards-Groves, C., Wilkinson, J., & Hardy, I. (2012). Ecologies of practices. In P. Hager, A. Lee, & A. Reich (Eds), *Practice, learning and change. Professional and practice-based learning*, (pp. 33–50), Springer.
Kemmis, S., Wilkinson, J., & Edwards-Groves, C. (2017). Roads not travelled, roads ahead: How the theory of practice architectures is travelling, Chapter 14. In K. Mahon, S. Francisco & S. Kemmis (Eds), *Exploring education and professional practice—Through the lens of practice architectures* (pp.239–256). Springer.
Kemmis, S., Wilkinson, J., Edwards-Groves, C., Hardy, I., Grootenboer, P., & Bristol, L. (2014). *Changing practices*. Springer.
Norris, J. (2022). *School leaders' sensemaking and sensegiving*. Brill.
Sachs, J. (2003). *The activist teaching profession*. Open university Press
Schatzki, T. R. (2002). *The site of the social: A philosophical account of the constitution of social life and change*. Pennsylvania State University Press.
Schatzki, T. R. (2010). *The timespace of human activity: On performance, society, and history as indeterminate teleological events*. Lexington.
Stetsenko, A. (2014). *Transformative activist stance for education: Inventing the future in moving beyond the status quo*. Springer.
Wilkinson, J. (2021). *Educational leadership through a practice lens: Practice matters*. Springer.

Appendix 1
Annotated Glossary

This annotated glossary has been prepared to provide readers with an accessible collection of key conceptual and technical terms important for understanding the theory of practice architectures and ecologies of practices. The table intends to support readers come to further clarity as they grapple with the ideas that the theory presents. Most of these concepts are related to other ideas and terms, but in the main have been in use since the theory was first published, noting their meanings have generally stood the test of time (although some ideas have been refined in their usage in reporting different empirical research). This glossary is annotated to provide more extended definitions and highlight important details and connections to other ideas raised in this book, and in previous writing, especially the early work—including:

Kemmis, S. (2010). Research for praxis: Knowing doing. *Pedagogy, Culture and Society*, 8(1), 9–27.

Kemmis, S. & Grootenboer, P. (2008). Situating praxis in practice: Practice architectures and the cultural, social and material conditions for practice. In S. Kemmis, & T. J. Smith (Eds.), *Enabling praxis: Challenges for education* (pp. 37–62). Sense Publishers.

Kemmis, S., Wilkinson, J., Edwards-Groves, C., Hardy, I., Grootenboer, P. & Bristol, L. (2014). *Changing practices, changing education*. Springer.

Schatzki, T. (1996). *Social practices: A Wittgensteinian approach to human activity and the social*. Cambridge University Press.

Schatzki, T. (2002). *The site of the social: A philosophical account of the constitution of social life and change*. The Pennsylvania State University Press.

Schatzki, T. (2003). A new societist social ontology. *Philosophy of the Social Sciences*, 33(2), 174–202.

Schatzki, T. (2010). *The timespace of human activity: On performance, society, and history as indeterminate teleological events*. Lexington.

We note and acknowledge that the table below builds on, and adapts, the Table of Key Terms originally published in:

Mahon, K., Kemmis, S., Francisco, S., & Lloyd, A. (2017). Introduction: Practice theory and the theory of practice architectures. In K. Mahon, S. Francisco & S. Kemmis (Eds.), *Exploring education and professional practice—Through the lens of practice architectures* (pp. 23–26). Springer.

Annotated Glossary: Main conceptual resources associated with the theory of practice architectures

Key concepts and terms	Definition/explanation
Cultural–discursive arrangements	The cultural and discursive arrangements formed by language, discourses, cultures and traditions, and that exist in, or are brought into, a site that enable and constrain the practice. This relates primarily, but not exclusively, to the *sayings* of a practice, by impacting what it is relevant and appropriate to say (and think) in performing, accomplishing, expressing, recounting, describing, interpreting, or justifying the practice
Doings	The realm of a practice that refers to what people are doing; that is, the delineation of what is being done, or the things done typical of a particular kind of practice and 'enacted' in characteristic modes of action, activity, and interactivity using particular kinds of material resources in the spaces in the sites where the practices are happening. Particular *doings* are carried, and understood, through work, participation and engaging in the activity of a particular practice at the time in a particular physical setting, space, or site
Ecologies of practices	*Ecologies of practices* form an integral part of the conceptual machinery of the theory of practice architectures and ecologies of practices; but importantly accounts for how practices are ecologically arranged (in practice arrangement bundles) amid broader exigencies and locally encountered contingencies. The connections between practices are empirically observable, and found in relationships and interrelationships in practices in a site
Education complex; practice complex; or complex of practices	This collection of terms refer to the dynamic traceable connections between broader complexes of practices; for example, in education the five practices of: (a) student learning, (b) teaching, (c) teacher learning, (d) leading, and (e) research and reflection form a complex in interrelated practices that can be said to be practice architectures for each of the others. The term 'practice complex' highlights the interplay between practices, practice architectures, and practicescapes and considers how practices in a complex of *practices* and practice architectures are inextricably related to, and exert influence on, one another

(continued)

Appendix 1: Annotated Glossary

(continued)

Key concepts and terms	Definition/explanation
Enabling and constraining/ enablements and constraints	To conceptualise the influences of practice architectures on practices and people (as practitioners of practices), close observation reveals that in a particular site, the practice architectures both *enable and constrain* simultaneously; that is, the practice architectures are not just *enablements* or just *constraints*, they, at the same time, enable some practices, and constrain others
Enmeshed (or enmeshment), entangled or entwined	The terms '*enmeshed*', '*enmeshment*', '*entangled*', and '*entwined*' are used to describe the close and intricately (indissoluble) connected web of relationships between practices and practice architectures; the words are sometimes used interchangeably
Hanging together (and bundling)	*Hanging together* is a term used to describe a state of inevitable and observable connectedness and co-existence between persons and practices as they are found 'bundled' together in the realities of participating (Schatzki, 1996). Relates to notions of practices being enmeshed in sites amid practice architectures (see also entry describing 'enmeshed, entangled or entwined' above)
Happeningness	*Happeningness* is a specific site ontological focus that centres on the dynamic motion and temporality of practices as they unfold or happen in real time activity and space. It denotes an intentional emphasis on the dynamic activity of participating in practices – not simply that they happen, but happen just as time passes moment-by-moment in sayings, doings and relatings as people come together in practices
Intersubjective space	The shared meaning making space that lies, and is created, between people (subjects) when they come together as interlocutors in practices to engage in interthinking, dialogue, shared activity and social relationships to make mutual understandings and consensus possible. This shared space for meaning making is called an *intersubjective space*. There are three interspatial dimensions creating an intersubjective space, these are semantic space (comprised of language, discourses and cultures), physical space-time (comprised of activity, interactivity and work), and social space (comprised of all things relational, where roles and relationships of power and solidarity influence agency, action and accomplishment of practices)
Material–economic arrangements	The material and economic arrangements formed by materiality, wealth, economic contingencies, physical spaces and available resources that exist in, or are brought into, a site, that enable and constrain the activity of a practice. This relates primarily, but not exclusively, to the doings of a practice, by affecting what, when, how, and by whom something can be done

(continued)

(continued)

Key concepts and terms	Definition/explanation
Meta-practices	*Meta-practices* are evident at the outer levels of the nested relationships, and although not often used currently, the notion of meta-practices (sometimes unhyphenated) can be used to denote broad macro level practices that shape or have directly bearing on other practices. Although it is true that many practices shape other practices, the term is useful to depict the macro-level practices that comprise a Practice Complex or Complex of Practices (see also the section above on Education complex); noting that whilst practices in a complex are discrete and can be analysed as such, these are also inherently interrelated
Niche	The term and concept of *niche* is a useful ecological metaphor describing the conditions of possibility and suitability for the existence and sustainability of a practice. Practices and practice architectures symbiotically and interdependently form conditions which sustain, or diminish, other practices within a particular *practicescape*. In this way, some practices can be 'hospitable' for other practices by creating suitable or 'niche' conditions and arrangements that enable them to occur in particular ways, and conversely, they can also be stifling of other practices, and constrain how they are able to happen and so might fall away. The niche of a practice is composed of the cultural-discursive, material-economic and social-political arrangements in a site that make a particular practice possible
Practice	A *practice* is a social activity and always, and at the same time, comprised of sayings, doings and relatings, where what is being said, being done and how people are relating to each other (in the moment of practicing) form a socially established cooperative human activity involving utterances and forms of understanding (sayings), activities, actions and interactions (doings), and ways in which people relate to one another and the world in relationships (relatings) that cohere or 'hang together' in characteristic ways in a distinctive 'project'

(continued)

Appendix 1: Annotated Glossary

(continued)

Key concepts and terms	Definition/explanation
Practice architectures	*Practice architectures* are the prefiguring conditions that exist in or are brought into a site, and so influence the practices that happen there. These conditions are configured as a complex formation and are cultural, interactional, linguistic, material, spatial, site-ontological, temporal, social, relational, and political in nature, and are experienced in practices as *cultural-discursive arrangements, material-economic arrangements, and social-political arrangements*. Practice architectures prefigure, but do not necessarily predetermine what happens in the moments of practicing. They always enable and constrain (and so influence, shape, mold or have bearing on) practices, and are understandable and/or made relevant in the sites where the practices are happening. 'Bundled' together, the three kinds of interrelated arrangements form practices architectures which give texture, contour and formation or shape to practices of one kind or another. Importantly, some practices can be practice architectures for other practices
Practice traditions	*Practice traditions* carry the historical imprints, remnants or traces of prior practices, and evident in sayings (displayed in language and discourses), doings (displayed in activities, physical set ups, the space and material resources being put to work), and ways of relating (display in the evidential power relationships, senses of agency and solidarity) as informing, influencing and organizing how practices happen in new occasions of practicing. They "encapsulate the history of the happenings of the practice … and act as a kind of collective 'memory' of the practice" (Kemmis, Wilkinson et al., 2014, p. 27). Practice traditions are experienced and locally understood in any practice and/or site (domestic, workplace, professional or community) when those people participating recognise that what is happening is 'how things work here' or 'the way we do things around here' (Kemmis et al., 2014)
Practicescapes	The term *practicescapes* encapsulates range of practices that comprise different practice sites, it extends Schatzki (2010) idea of, practice landscapes refers to practice settings (e.g., early childhood centres, hospitals, TAFE Institutes, schools) where multiple kinds of different practices occur, and in which there may be multiple and overlapping sites of practice. The term encompasses the people who are emplaced in the setting, the practices that are enacted there, the practice architectures that give the setting its character, and the practice traditions that have been established in the setting over time. It encompasses the relationships between practices, practice architectures, and practice traditions within, and constituting, the setting

(continued)

(continued)

Key concepts and terms	Definition/explanation
Praxis/Praxis-oriented	In the theory of practice architectures, the terms *praxis* and *praxis-oriented* tie practitioners to practices by adding a sense of moral purpose, intention and ethical conduct to understanding practices. The concepts draw on "both a neo-Aristotelian sense to denote "action that is morally-committed, and oriented and informed by traditions in a field" (Kemmis & Smith, 2008, p. 4) and in a post Hegelian and post Marxian sense to denote "history making action" (Kemmis, 2010a, p. 9)" (cited in Mahon et al., 2017, p.25)
Prefigure, prefiguring, prefigurements	Practice architectures enable and constrain what is possible in a practice–in this way they can foreshadow or *prefigure* how a practice unfolds in a site. It is important to note that *prefiguring* does not mean predetermining – noting that the practitioner always has some agency within what is possible vis-à-vis the practice architectures. What is and can be done, spoken about and how people in different interpersonal, and so political, relationships relate to one another (there and then in a practice) is/can be pre-figured by conditions already present, for example: i) history, ethnic, racial and social cultures, the dominant or additional languages present/expected, models or programs, experiences, policies and practice traditions; ii) the physical arrangements or configurations and set-ups already laid out in a space (e.g., furniture, room layout) and the material resources and objects available and in use in a practice setting (in a room or building); and iii) the understood/accepted/expected authorities and balances of power and relational intensities present (e.g. doctor-patient, teacher-student, financial advisor-client). These contingencies prefigure practices and practice architectures influencing, but not necessarily determining, what is and can be done, spoken about and how the social relationships are encountered and/or developed
Project (as in the project of a practice)	The *project of a practice* can be understood in terms of what is legitimately and intuitively answered in response to the question "what are you doing?" or "what is happening here?" Specifically, a project is comprised of 'teleoaffective structures' (Schatzki, 2002) informed by the aims, actions and practices, and individual and collective accomplishments (ends)
Relatings	The realm of a practice that refers to relationality and how people are relating to one another and the world around them; that is, the delineation of the characteristic ways individuals in their discourses, activity and interactivity relate to one another. *Relatings* are carried, and understood, through different kinds of relationships, often prefigured by predetermined roles, personal and collective agency and solidarity, and power as experienced in these social relationships

(continued)

Appendix 1: Annotated Glossary

(continued)

Key concepts and terms	Definition/explanation
Sayings	The realm of a practice that refers to what people are saying and thinking; that is, the delineation of what is being said in terms of the discourses used, and the ideas being communicated discursively and interpreted in characteristic and coherent forms of understanding, speaking, and thinking. *Sayings* are carried, and understood, multimodally through expressed language and representations of thoughts, words and ideas (for example through alphabetic symbols used in the English language in texts)
Sayings, doings, and relatings	The always interconnected actions of which practices are comprised. *Sayings* include utterances, thought and forms of understandings; *doings* include physical actions and activity; and *relatings* include ways in which people relate to one another and the world. In practices, sayings, doings, and relatings hang together, and so, are always bundled as they unfold in real time activity. See also separate sections of each realm
Semantic space, physical space–time, and social space	These are the three interspatial interrelated dimensions of intersubjective space (found present in a site) where interlocutors encounter one another as shared meaning makers in and through their practices. *Semantic space* attends to how people make sense of one another as interlocutors, in the medium of language; *physical space-time* refers to the physical and material space where people encounter one another and other things in the world as embodied beings at a particular time, in the medium of activity and work; *social space* considers the sociality, and so the relationality, of encounter between people as social beings, in the medium of individual and collective agency, solidarity and power
Site	A *site* refers to the specific place or local setting where a practice is happening; however, we acknowledge that a classroom can be a site equally as the school site where the classroom is located. Schatzki (2003), also states that the site of a practice is "that realm or set of phenomena (if any) of which it is intrinsically a part" (p. 176). In response to the multiple contextual meanings of site, we adapt Schatzki's notion of differentiating three interconnected "senses of the site" (2002, p. 63-64) as important in providing a more comprehensive account of the realities of understanding the complexity of sites, and so what a site ontological perspective means: the *first sense of site* focuses on the specific, immediate, spatial location where practices occur; the *second sense of site* concerns the wider context or local realm in which practices exist, and the *third sense of site* relates to the broader space, field, or domain which the practice is intrinsically located

(continued)

(continued)

Key concepts and terms	Definition/explanation
Site based practice development	This concept provides a way of conceptualising practice development as necessarily local, and in doing so rejects the notion of best practice, which is often seen as a singular universal practice that brings about growth and development, regardless of the particularities of the site. It is argued that *site based practice development* (usually unhyphenated in this usage) makes sustainable transformation possible since knowing and responding to the site is central
Site ontological	The *site ontological* perspective is a key feature of the theory of practice architectures which acknowledges the distinctive local conditions and circumstances that influence the conduct of practices, and focuses interest on the particularity of how, when, what, why and that practices are happening in a particular place at a particular time
Social–political arrangements	The social and political arrangements, formed by roles, relationships, senses and experiences of agency, solidarity and power that exist in, or are brought into, a site, that enable and constrain the interpersonal relationality of a practice. This relates primarily, but not exclusively, to the relatings of a practice, by shape how people relate in a practice to other people and to non-human objects
Stirred into practices/learning	The notion of being '*stirred in*' is intended to (metaphorically) capture dynamic ways people become practitioners of practices through processes of participating in a practice; the imagery implies a sense of temporality and specificity as people become initiated into practices. In other words, it creates a sense of how and that people learn to continue on in a practice. This term is used to describe ways people are being stirred into the very particular sayings, doings and ways of relating that comprise a practice of one kind or another
Table of invention	A *table of invention* is a research tool that can be used to collate data and organise the analysis of data using the theory of practice architectures by: first, having the analyst delineate then record the particular dimensions of practice (in terms of what is being said, what is being done, and how interlocutors are relating to one another); second, providing a frame for recording the particular enabling and constraining conditions or practice architectures (in terms of the cultural-discursive, material-economic and social-political arrangements) that are influencing what happens/is happening in the reported accounts, observations etc; third, recording other relevant information gleaned from the data (e.g., personal attributes, preliminary themes, the project of the practice observed)

Index

A
Accounts of practice, 51, 53
Action research, 55
Actuality of practice, 49
Agency, x, 1, 3, 7, 9, 12, 27, 51, 59, 66, 67, 90, 95, 97, 100
Aristotle, 73
Artefacts of practice, 50

B
Bourdieu, 76

C
Capra, 38
Case study, 54
Changing practices, changing education, vii, ix, x, 34, 55, 73, 93
Coding, 71
Critical ethnography, 55
Cultural-discursive, 1, 11, 21, 27, 32, 37, 42, 47, 50, 57, 59, 60–62, 69, 71–73, 75, 76, 81, 83, 89, 94, 96, 97

D
Design-based research, 55
Discourses, vii, viii, 10, 13, 19, 22, 44, 50, 59, 61, 62, 66, 68, 71, 72, 87
Dispositions, 73, 81
Dissemination, ix, 39, 67, 79, 83, 85–91
Doings, 16

E
Ecologies of practices, ix, x, 25, 27, 28, 30, 32–34, 36, 38, 41, 44, 46, 53, 55, 73, 80, 93, 94
Education, v, 73
Education Complex, ix, 28, 34, 35, 37
Edwards-Groves, vi, viii–xi, 3, 10–13, 15, 21, 26, 29, 30, 45, 49, 52, 55, 57, 60, 65, 66, 68, 72, 79, 80, 83, 84–87, 90, 93
Enable and constrain, 10, 12, 16, 17–19, 21, 22, 27, 35, 42, 46, 51, 53, 55, 58, 74, 88, 94, 95, 98, 100
Enmeshed, 75

F
Feel for the game, 76
Freebody, 3, 48, 49, 51, 52, 53, 58, 60, 65, 66, 72, 86

G
Gherardi, viii, 45
Green, viii
Grootenboer, vi, viii–x, 2, 3, 10, 12–15, 21, 25–28, 32, 33, 35, 45, 62, 72, 79, 87, 93

H
Habitus, 76
Hadot, viii
Hang together, 6, 74, 75
Happeningness, 3, 10, 13, 15, 20–22, 41, 43, 45, 47, 49, 52, 53, 55, 59, 72, 80, 95

Happenings, vi, 9, 13, 14, 15, 60, 97
Hardy, 57, 93
History, 73, 76, 80

I
Interaction analysis, 57, 61, 62, 70, 71
Intersubjective meaning making, 7, 68, 82
Intersubjective space, vii, 1, 3, 7, 18, 19, 81, 95
Interviews, 22, 51, 52, 54, 60–62, 65, 66, 73, 82, 89

K
Kemmis, viii, 79, 98
Knorr-Cetina, viii
Knowledge, 4, 8, 21, 22, 30, 42, 43, 45, 54, 63, 67, 69, 70, 76, 86, 87, 89, 90

M
MacIntyre, viii
Material-economic, 1, 10–13, 16–19, 21, 27, 32, 37, 42, 47, 50, 57, 60–62, 71–73, 75, 81, 83, 89, 95, 97, 100
Methodologies, 54

P
Particular, 21
Pedagogy Education and Praxis (PEP), ix, x, xiii, 86
Philosophical-empirical inquiry, 84
Physical space-time, 1, 10, 18, 19, 26, 61, 72, 81, 82, 89, 90, 95, 99
Power, 1, 4, 7, 10, 12, 18, 19, 36, 51, 59, 67, 68, 76, 84, 90, 100
Power and *solidarity*, 76
Practice architectures, 71–73, 79
Practice arrangement bundles, 11, 25, 27, 38, 73, 80
Practice complex, 33
Practice landscape, 75
Practicescapes, 1, 12, 13, 22, 25, 27–29, 31, 37, 38, 73, 79–81, 87, 88, 97
Practice theories, 1–5, 20, 41, 45, 58
Practice traditions, 9, 13, 14, 35, 46, 59, 71, 76, 98
Practice webs, 63
Practitioners of practices, 5, 25, 31, 38, 41, 57, 67, 81
Prefigures, 13
Prefiguring, 69, 70, 85, 98

Project, 7

R
Reading Recovery™, 8
Reckwitz, viii
Relatings, 6
Research questions, vi, 42, 49, 53, 54, 66, 72
Rönnerman, 57

S
Sayings, 7
Schatzki, viii, 7, 11, 27, 42, 43, 80, 85, 97
Schooling, vii, 33, 34
Self-determination, vi
Self-development, vi
Self-expression, vi
Semantic, vi, viii, 3, 7, 10, 11, 18, 19, 44, 61, 72, 81, 89, 90, 95, 99
Semantic space, 81
Sensemaking, 10, 11, 59, 81, 90
Shotter, viii
Site, 9, 10, 47, 81, 82
Site ontological, x, 1, 3, 12–16, 20–22, 26, 41–43, 45–49, 52–55, 58, 59, 74, 80, 82, 85, 88, 91, 95, 100
Site-based practice development, 25
Situatedness, 21, 22, 37, 39, 41, 42, 45, 48, 53
Skills, 76
Smith, 93, 98
Social constructivist, 73
Sociality, vi, 1, 2, 44, 80, 84, 88, 99
Social-political, 1, 7, 10–13, 15–19, 21, 27, 32, 37, 42, 47, 50, 57, 59, 60, 62, 70–73, 81, 83, 90, 96, 97, 100
Social-political arrangements, 27, 97
Social space, 81
Solidarity, 4, 7, 9, 10, 18, 19, 51, 59, 76, 95, 97–100
Study design, 53

T
Table of invention, 50, 57, 68, 69, 72, 73, 75, 100
Teleoaffective structures, 7
Thematic analysis, 71
Three senses of site, 44, 48
Time-space of human activity, 5
Transcripts, 49, 50, 53, 62, 63, 65–68, 71, 72, 74, 75, 82

Index

Transformation, vi, vii, x, 15, 37, 79, 81, 85, 88, 89, 91, 100

V
Values, 76
Von Savigny, viii

Vygotsky, viii

W
Wilkinson, viii, ix, xi, 79, 87, 93, 97
Wittgenstein, viii

SPRINGER NATURE

GPSR Compliance

The European Union's (EU) General Product Safety Regulation (GPSR) is a set of rules that requires consumer products to be safe and our obligations to ensure this.

If you have any concerns about our products, you can contact us on ProductSafety@springernature.com

In case Publisher is established outside the EU, the EU authorized representative is:

Springer Nature Customer Service Center GmbH
Europaplatz 3
69115 Heidelberg, Germany

The manufacturer's authorised representative in the EU is Springer Nature Customer Service Centre GmbH, Europaplatz 3, 69115 Heidelberg, Germany. If you have any concerns regarding our products, please contact ProductSafety@springernature.com

Printed and bound by CPI Group (UK) Ltd, Croydon, CR0 4YY

23/03/2026

02076398-0014